The Peakland Way

75p

By the same author:

EXPLORE DERBYSHIRE BY CAR

FAMOUS DERBYSHIRE HOMES

LEGENDS OF DERBYSHIRE

PEAK DISTRICT WALKS—

1. Short Walks for the Motorist
2. Long Walks for the Rambler

The Peakland Way

96 miles through the Peak District National Park

by

John N. Merrill

Dalesman Books
1975

The Dalesman Publishing Company Ltd.,
Clapham (via Lancaster), North Yorkshire
First published 1975

ISBN: 0 85206 260 5

Printed and Bound in Great Britain by
Ellesmere Press Ltd., Mill Lane, Skipton, North Yorkshire

Contents

Illustrations

The front cover photograph is of Hathersage.

The photographs on page 33 and the back cover are courtesy Sheffield Telegraph. All other photographs, and the maps, are by the author.

Preface

THE Peak District is famed for its unique beauty and contrasting landscape. The Peakland Way is a 96 mile circular long distance walk around the Peak District National Park. The Way takes in the different types of scenery that make up the region, the limestone dales, the gritstone moorlands and thc gritstone edges. Interwoven with the places that you pass through are descriptions of legends, traditions, interesting buildings, historical features and a wide range of flowers and birds. The route takes you to the lesser known places of the Peak District—this does not mean that the places are not as beautiful or interesting, rather the reverse. In fact, I would go as far as to say that you will be surprised at the places you see and learn about.

The route and idea of the Way has been my own and I can only hope that you enjoy walking it as much as I do. The inaugural crossing of the Peakland Way I did myself between 10th August and 15th August 1973. I set off in perfect weather with hardly a cloud in the sky. For the subsequent days as I walked round the sun shone every day and it made the task a pleasure. I can only hope that on your crossing you will experience the same perfect conditions. It is hoped to form a Peakland Way Club which would meet once a year at a certain Peak District hostelry. Here Peakland Wayers could enjoy a meal, the like of which they never ate on the Way itself. Membership of the club would be only open to persons completing the circular walk. To all of you who do the walk, please write to me letting me know your names and addresses, and dates of your crossing so that I can keep an accurate record of fellow Peakland Wayers.

May I wish you the very best of luck on your walk, and look forward to seeing you in the near future.

JOHN N. MERRILL,
6 Farwater Close, Dronfield,
Sheffield S18 6RE.

Introduction

The Route

The Peakland Way is a circular walk around the Peak District National Park and is traversed in a clockwise direction. The whole of the 96 mile walk is along rights-of-way. Many are signposted and almost without exception stone stiles exist where necessary. Linking the footpaths together about five miles of road walking is necessary, spread over the entire route. The walking instructions and maps included in this book are intended to be complementary to a one-inch or 2½-inch map and not to be used on their own. There is only one way to walk round and that is with map in hand and constant checking of your route. This will ensure that you do not wander off course. Many of the footpaths, at the time of writing, are little used. This means that although signs and stiles are there, the path in between is often not discernible. This is an advantage because you know you are "off the beaten track."

The aim of the historical and nature notes in the book is to give the walker information on the places he passes through. It also gives an incentive and purpose for walking in the countryside as many of the places and items mentioned can only be seen on foot. The notes on birds and flowers are from my own observations while walking the Way.

Maps

The whole of the Way is covered on the one-inch O.S. Tourist Edition, "The Peak District", and on Sheet No. 111, "Buxton and Matlock." The 2½-inch maps for the entire walk are sheet Nos. SK14, SK15, SK05, SK06, SK16, SK17, SK18, SK08, SK19, SK28, SK27, SK26, and SK25. The 2½-inch O.S. Map, "The Dark Peak", covers the whole of Kinder section of the Way.

Equipment

The secret of carrying your equipment is to go as lightweight as possible so that your load becomes a joy and not a burden. Between 25-30 lbs. weight is ample. Stout boots, anorak, two shirts, underclothes, four pairs of socks (two thick, two thin), pullover, sleeping bag, tent, cooking utensils, stove, tin opener, spoon, whistle, compass, matches, torch, towel, soap and toothpaste are the essentials. I find a spoon is all you need to eat with. Instead of plates I find it better to eat out of the cooking pan. Carry no water as you can obtain this from where you stay.

Food

Carry two or three days food with you all the time. Villages are few so stock up when you can. Dehydrated food is naturally the norm, being light and compact. A suggested day's meal which I use on all my long walks is:—

Breakfast—Alpen style cereal or porridge. Mug of coffee.
Lunch—An orange and a bar of fruit and nut chocolate.
Dinner—One pint packet of soup. Irish Stew. Small tin of fruit. Coffee and biscuits.

Accommodation

Although the route is primarily written for walkers carrying everything on their back, there is nothing to stop Youth Hostelers and others from doing the walk. Other forms of accommodation are either located on or close to the Way. Many inns and villagers offer accommodation and most farmers are willing to let the occasional camper pitch his tent in one of their fields. There is no camp site at Blackwell (end of Stage Two), but many of the farmers there allow campers. No official camp site exists in the Hathersage area and for the end of Stage Five you must seek alternative accommodation or use the Youth Hostel.

Prior permission is necessary to use the camp site or hostel run by the Peak Park Planning Board at Hagg Farm. Write to the Warden at the address below, stating the date and number of tents to be pitched. The site has a capacity of 15. The hostel has accommodation for 18 women and 18 men. A deposit is necessary to confirm the booking.

Addresses of camp sites at the end of Way stages

Stage One:-	Mr. J. Grindey, Wetton Mill, Wetton, Nr. Ashbourne, Derbyshire DE6 2AG.
Stage Two:-	Blackwell village—see general notes.
Stage Three:-	Mrs. A. Cooper, Waterside Farm, Barber Booth, Edale, Derbyshire.
Stage Four:-	The Warden, Hagg Farm, Ashopton, Bamford, Sheffield, S30 2BJ.

Stage Five:-	Stay in Hathersage, where there is a Youth Hostel.
Stage Six:-	Mr. C. W. Smedley, Moorside Farm, Robin Hood, Baslow, Bakewell, Derbyshire.
Stage Seven:-	Mr. Bailey, Dudwood House, Winster, Matlock, Derbyshire.

Villages with camp sites on or close to the Way

Wetton, Hulme End, Longnor, Buxton, Rowter Farm ($1\frac{1}{2}$ miles south-west of Castleton), Edale, Snake Pass, Hope, Grindleford, Calver, Birchover, Ashbourne.

Youth Hostels on or close to the Way

Ilam Hall, Hartington, Buxton, Ravenstor, Castleton, Edale, Hathersage, Bakewell, Elton.

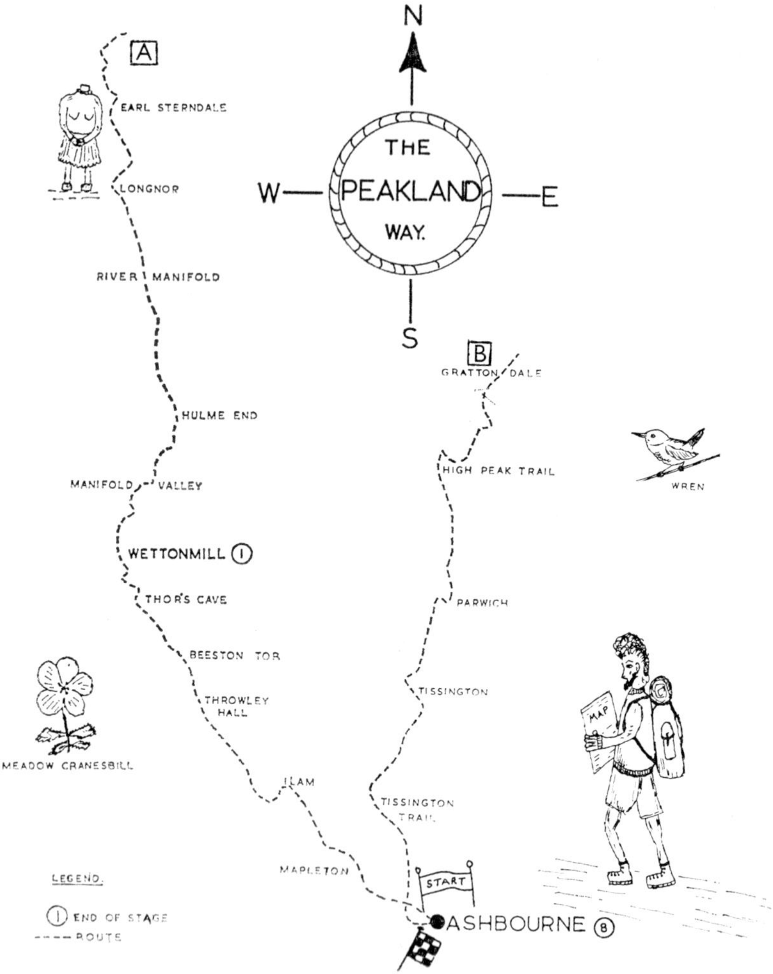

The Peakland Way:

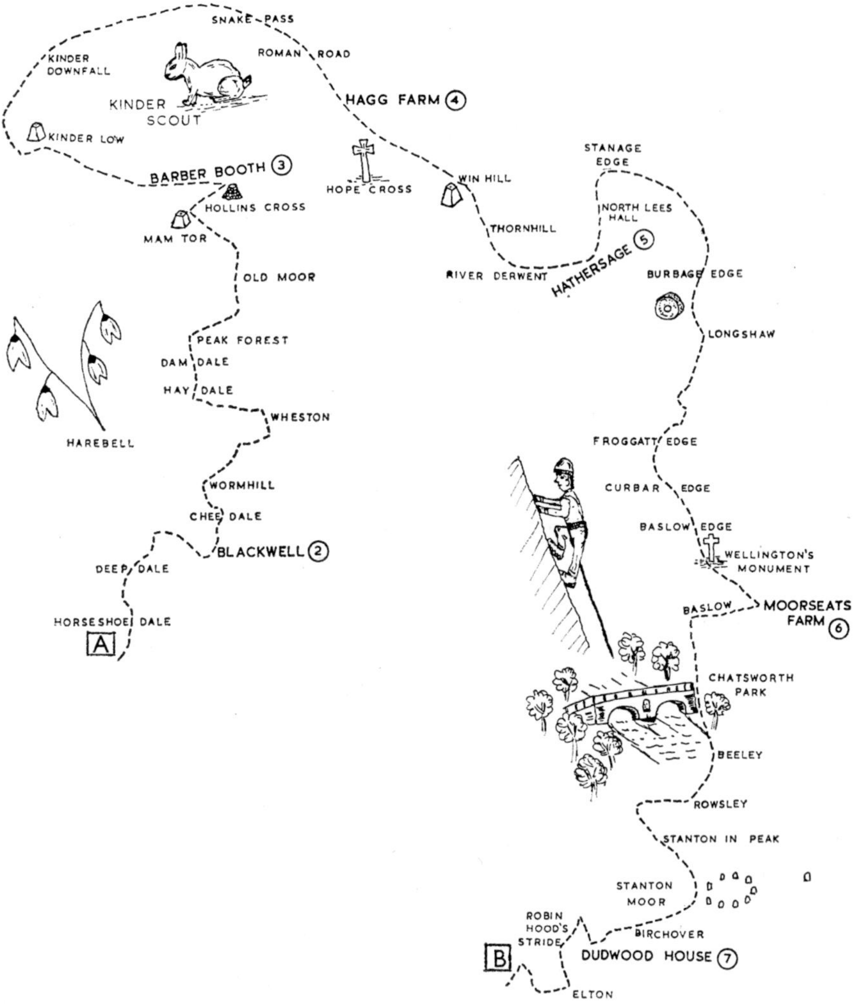

General Route Map

Part One

The Peakland Way stage by stage

Stage One: Ashbourne to Wettonmill

Route:— *Ashbourne — Mapleton — Littlepark — Coldwall Bridge — Ilam — Musden Grange — Throwley Hall — Beeston Tor — Weag's Bridge — Thor's Cave — Wettonmill.*
Distance:— 10 *miles.*
$2\frac{1}{2}$*-inch O.S. Maps:—* *Sheet Nos. SK* 06, *SK* 16, *SK* 05 *and SK* 15.

You are about to set off and circle one of the most interesting and beautiful areas in England. Granted your feet will be sore, the odd blister or two will appear, your muscles will ache and your shoulders moan from the weight of your rucksack, but it is all in a good cause. Away from the modern trappings of life you will enter a week of peace, papers won't be read, the radio won't be heard, only the smell and noise of the countryside will accompany you on your walk. Is there anything finer?

This, the first stage, is short and makes a good introduction to the journey ahead. If you have time do look around Ashbourne before you start, but preferably leave this till the end when you can wander around at leisure and see its many treasures. You begin the walk from the cross in the cobbled Market Square. Having traditionally touched the cross, stride out and cross Union Street to the public lavatories. Keep these on your left and ascend the cobbled footpath named "The Channel." This path is the only piece you will walk twice. At the top, cross the road and as signposted — "Footpath to Dovedale"—follow the stiles down across the fields to the river Bradbourne. Cross the footbridge over the river and walk under the second railway bridge. Above is the disused railway line which is now converted into the Tissington Trail. This you will walk along at the end of the Way.

Just round the other side of the bridge, turn left at the kissing gate and ascend the fields, using the wooden stiles. As you begin to descend the other side the village of Mapleton can be seen, and about halfway down the hillside bear right and head for the centre of the village. The footpath runs between the houses and you reach the road, just to the left of the *Okeover Arms*. Virtually opposite on

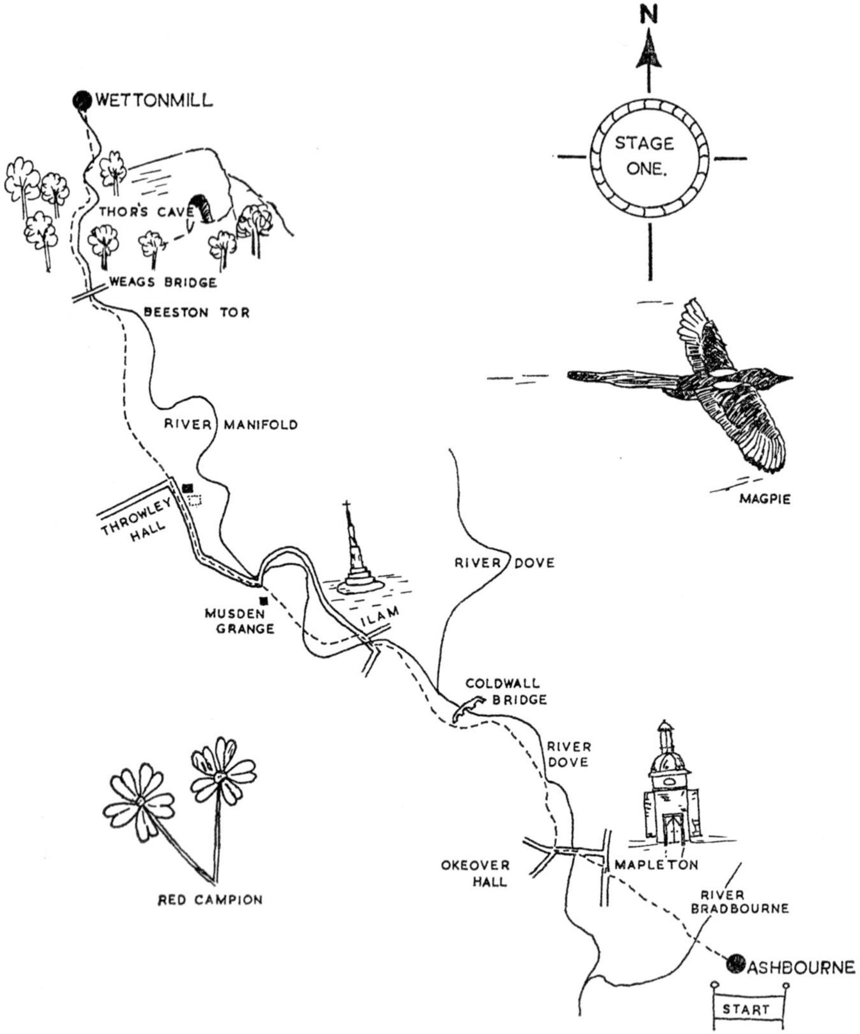
N
STAGE ONE.
WETTONMILL
THOR'S CAVE
WEAGS BRIDGE
BEESTON TOR
MAGPIE
RIVER MANIFOLD
THROWLEY HALL
RIVER DOVE
MUSDEN GRANGE
ILAM
COLDWALL BRIDGE
RIVER DOVE
OKEOVER HALL
MAPLETON
RIVER BRADBOURNE
RED CAMPION
ASHBOURNE
START

your left you can see the signpost for the path across the field to the bridge over the river Dove. Before you follow this, do visit Mapleton church which is dedicated to St. Mary. It is very unusual with a pillared porch and a tower capped by an octagonal dome with a lantern on top. The original church fell into decay and about 1750 the current building, which is only 52 ft. 8 ins. long and 17 ft. wide, was erected. Some of the glass inside came from the original church and the five beams which support the flat roof are believed to be from the earlier building.

Leave Mapleton via the footpath on your left across the field to the bridge over the river Dove. Continue along the road from the bridge and cross another bridge before you turn right and walk past a mill on your right. A signpost indicates the way, saying "Ilam 2½ miles." Just in front of the mill in July and August the water's edge is clustered with yellow monkey flowers and around the fringe are the tall red flowers of great willow herb, a plant you will often see on the Way. The mill is unusual and similar to another you will see much further up the Manifold river on Stage Two. The water wheel, instead of being characteristically on the outside, is in the centre of the building.

At the point where you leave the road to walk along the footpath past the mill you are opposite the driveway to Okeover Hall. The building is not open to the public. The Okeover family have lived on this site since 1150 when Ralph Fitzormus De Okeover was granted the land by the Abbot of Burton. The current occupier is Sir Ian Walker-Okeover, who is Lord Lieutenant of Derbyshire. The present building dates from 1780 and is constructed from red brick and faced with stone. Leake Okeover began building it during his lifetime, 1701-1765. Over the subsequent generations it was added to but it was left to the present owner to tidy and complete the original plan, which he did in the 1950s.

Keep to the left hand side of the mill and, although the path is faint, the stiles will guide you. First you hug the side of the river before heading across the field to the lane just south of Littlepark Farm. Where you leave the river, about a quarter of a mile from the mill, you will see on your left in the summer a small group of beautiful blue nettled-leaved bellflowers. You will see several of these in many places at different points of the Way. On reaching the lane turn right, and in front of the Littlepark Farm turn left before bearing right and passing a hollowed oak tree on your left before heading down to the river Dove through a small plantation. You curve round the field beyond before entering another wood. Here red campion grows in profusion, and you should also see tufted vetch and a few clusters of wood vetch, generally a white or pink flower with blue veins. It is one of the rarer members of the vetch family, of which there are five in Britain.

Shortly after emerging from the wood you are confronted by and are probably surprised to see a substantial bridge, known as Coldwall Bridge. It bears the date 1726 and formed part of a coach road which is hardly discernible today. It stretches for 100 yards and at the other end, close to Thorpe village, there is a milestone recording that it is eleven miles to Cheadle. It is sad to see such a magnificent construction left to itself. At the bridge turn left as signposted and right almost immediately afterwards, and a quarter of a mile later you are beside the Dove which you keep close to you for nearly a mile to Ilam village.

This particular stretch to Ilam is delightful walking. Harebells, meadow cranesbill, tormentil and foxgloves grow in profusion. Butterflies such as green streaked white, red admiral and small tortoiseshell flit effortlessly from flower to flower. The birds are busy too with wood pigeons in the trees. Magpies startle you as they hop over walls or fly up in front of you and, on my inaugural walk, I flushed a grey heron. On the river itself mallards hurry to the other side or take off clumsily, and moorhens utter their abrupt call giving away their whereabouts. Alas, this idyllic bliss is shattered as you reach the bridge on its left-hand side and gain the road and village of Ilam.

Turn right and cross the bridge and straight in front of you is Ilam Cross, which stands 30 ft. high and was built by Jesse Watts-Russell in memory of his wife in 1840. At the cross turn left and a little higher up the road you can turn left again and follow the fenced path to Ilam church, beyond which is Ilam Hall. In the 1840s when Jesse Watts-Russell was building the hall you see today (although a good proportion of it has been dismantled) he also completely rebuilt the village. The Tudor Gothic building is now a Youth Hostel and was given to the National Trust in 1934 by Sir Robert McDougall. During the 17th century the hall was owned by the Congreve family. One of them, William Congreve, who at the age of 18 had been very ill, came here to recuperate. To keep his mind occupied he spent much of his time in a grotto in the grounds where he wrote the once famous comedy. "The Old Bachelor." Another writer, Samuel Johnson, also knew Ilam well and to help pay for his mother's funeral and her debts he wrote his only novel, *Rasselas*, which he set around Ilam. Working in the evenings, he wrote the whole book of 45,000 words in one week!

The church, dedicated to the Holy Cross, is well worth visiting as it has links with other places you will see later on this stage of the walk. Although there is evidence of the Saxon building, the tower base is 13th century, the South Chapel was added in 1618 and most of the building was restored by Sir Gilbert Scott in 1884. The South Chapel is the most interesting part. It contains a 13th century monument to St. Bertram, who was active in the 8th century and lived and worked in this area. Close to Ilam is St. Bertram's Well and a cave at Beeston Tor is known as St. Bertram's Cave. He was a son of a King of Mercia, but because he had abandoned his princely life—following the death of his daughter and wife from wolves—his self-sacrifice was renowned. Pilgrims came from all over to visit his tomb and many would lie on top of it hoping for a cure.

Also in the South Chapel is the alabaster tomb of Robert Meverell, who died in 1626, and his wife. They lived in the now ruined Throwley Hall which you will pass soon. Over the doorway to the chapel can be seen the initials R.M. for Richard Meverell, the owner of Throwley; R.P. for Rowe Port, the owner of Ilam Hall; and N.H. for Nicholas Hurt, the owner of Castern just north-west of Ilam. An octagonal chapel was added in 1884 and this houses the elaborate white sculptured tomb of 1826 by Francis Chantery to David Pike Watts. Outside in the graveyard can be seen the shafts of two 10th century Saxon crosses.

In front of the hall turn left, descend the steps and head down to the river Manifold to follow the wide path beside it. A little way along here you will pass another shaft of a Saxon cross which is locally known as the Battle Stone. When Jesse Watts-Russell was rebuilding the village in 1840, he found this stone incorporated into a house which he was having pulled down. He saved it and had it placed here. This section beside the river Manifold is known as "Paradise Walk," mainly because of its setting. The wide river sweeps round gracefully, flowers grow in abundance along its edge, trees drape their branches into the water and brown trout swim gaily along. In the summer the river bubbles up from the ground a little further up, after travelling along subterranean passageways from Wettonmill, six miles away. Only in winter with the increased rainfall does the river run all the way down above ground. The rock is limestone which accounts for the water's disappearing tricks.

Approximately half a mile from the hall you come to a footbridge over the river. Here turn left and cross it before bearing half right across the fields, keeping to the right-hand side of Musden Grange. All the stiles are there but the path is rarely trodden. Close to a farm building you attain the single-tracked road. Here turn left and right immediately afterwards, and follow the road for a little over a mile as it weaves its way and gradually ascends to Throwley Hall. Standing forlornly in front of the 19th century hall are the ruins of the earlier building. This was built in about 1603 by Sampson Meverell from the stone of an even earlier structure.

Follow the road through the farm and at the other side leave it and turn right. On your left is the stile, and the path through the trees and then the field. Traverse the field, going close to the wall of another on your right, before gaining the hill and the centre of a stretched "Z"-shaped wood. Here you will find a wooden ladder stile. Once over this descend and below in the bottom you can see a track. Head down to this and continue down it to Beeston Tor

Farm. As you do so you can see in front one of the largest limestone buttresses in the Peak District, Beeston Tor. It rises to a height of 200 ft. and extends for approximately 600 ft.

Apart from containing several awkward and difficult rock climbs up the face, there are some interesting caves which have yielded many archaeological finds. At the base of Beeston Tor is St. Bertram's Cave. It is an easy cave to explore and for about 600 ft. you can crawl your way along, although it is often muddy. The animal bones, and other finds from the cave, can be seen in the Buxton and British Museums. In September 1924 the Rev. G. H. Wilson found a hoard of fifty Saxon silver coins, which are believed to have been deposited here in about 871 A.D. About 140 ft. up the limestone face is Lynx Cave. It is possible to reach this, but the ascent is exposed and only able persons should climb to it. The cave is 150 ft. long, and the reason for its name is that only the bones from the lynx have been found in it. These are now on display in the Natural History Museum in London. Just to the right is the Lower Lynx Cave, where polecat and reindeer bones have been found.

From Beeston Tor Farm turn left and follow the track. From Weag's Bridge you go along the tarmacadamed trackbed of the Leek and Manifold Light Railway all the way to Wettonmill. The railway was the last to be constructed in the Peak District. Work began in March 1902 and was completed two years later, the line being officially opened on 27th June 1904. The railway ran from the village of Waterhouses at the southern end of the Hamps Valley and ended at Hulme End, approximately nine miles due north in the Manifold Valley. The gauge was narrow, being only 2 ft. 6 ins., and the cost of construction was £4,292 per mile. Two engines named "E. R. Calthrop" and "J. P. Earle"—after the engineers—pulled yellow coaches which were Indian in style with verandas.

The purpose of the line was to carry mining and quarry traffic, milk from the Ecton creamery and also tourists, as all the footpaths were along the summit of the valley. One station was just north of Beeston Tor. Another at Weag's Bridge was known as Grindon; it is now a car park. Another was at the foot of Thor's Cave, a further one existed at the next road junction from Wetton and was known as Redhurst, and Wettonmill had a station where the car park is today. The line was never a financial success, and it was only due to the tourist trade that it remained open as long as it did. On 10th March 1934 the train traversed the railway for the last time. Work began on dismantling everything and it was decided that the line should be made a gift to the Staffordshire County Council. It converted the railway at a cost of £6,000 into the public footpath which you are walking along today.

At Weag's Bridge continue straight ahead on the tarmacadamed surface and follow the gentle curving track as it meanders through the woodland—hence the name Manifold Valley. Beside you knapweed, cow parsley, small scabious, yellow pansies and different varieties of dandelion sway in the cool breeze. In the trees nuthatch are frequently seen in the summer and more often than not you will hear and see that beautiful small songster, the wren. With its short cocked tail, it will flit through the branches in front of you.

On rounding a corner, and on your right near the summit of the valley side, stands the huge limestone buttress and yawning entrance of Thor's Cave. Down at its base is a wooden bridge, where you can leave your rucksack and ascend the path for 300 ft. It is worth it for the view but also to see the large proportions of the cave. The entrance you walk through is 30 ft. high and 23 ft. wide. In the middle of the last century Samuel Carrington, the schoolmaster of nearby Wetton, found arrow heads, bone combs and pins, iron adzes, spindle wheels and bronze armillae in the cave. These confirm that it was occupied by Celts, Romans and Anglo-Saxons. The finds can be seen in both Derby and Sheffield (Weston Park) Museums.

Thirty feet to the south of the west window of Thor's Cave is Thor's Fissure Cave. In the late 1920s and early '30s, the Rev. G. H. Wilson and his son excavated this cave. They removed two tons of earth and found an incredible range of animal bones which included bear, deer, reindeer, ox, goat, sheep, pig, fox, wolf, horse, polecat and a dolphin. They also uncovered human bones and many objects used by early man.

Descend to the bridge and your abandoned rucksack. Just before you cross, over on your left is another cave known as Donkey Cave or Radcliffe Stables. According to tradition a person named Radcliffe stabled his horse here in 1745 when the Young Pretender was in the country, so that it wouldn't be taken for his cause. Continue along the track, cross the road from Wetton and shortly afterwards you see the tents and the building of Wettonmill, formerly a corn mill which ceased operation at the end of the last century. At Wettonmill you will see the river flowing once more. The Manifold disappears close by down a swallet and reappears, as you saw earlier, near Ilam.

You have completed the first stage. Now you can relax, quench your thirst and feed your ravenous stomach. Wettonmill is a grand place to camp and end a walk. The river trickles by with trout and grayling in it. The sun casts her shadows, monkey flowers and forget-me-nots bloom along the bankside and tame chaffinches approach seeking a morsel. Yes, it is a perfect place.

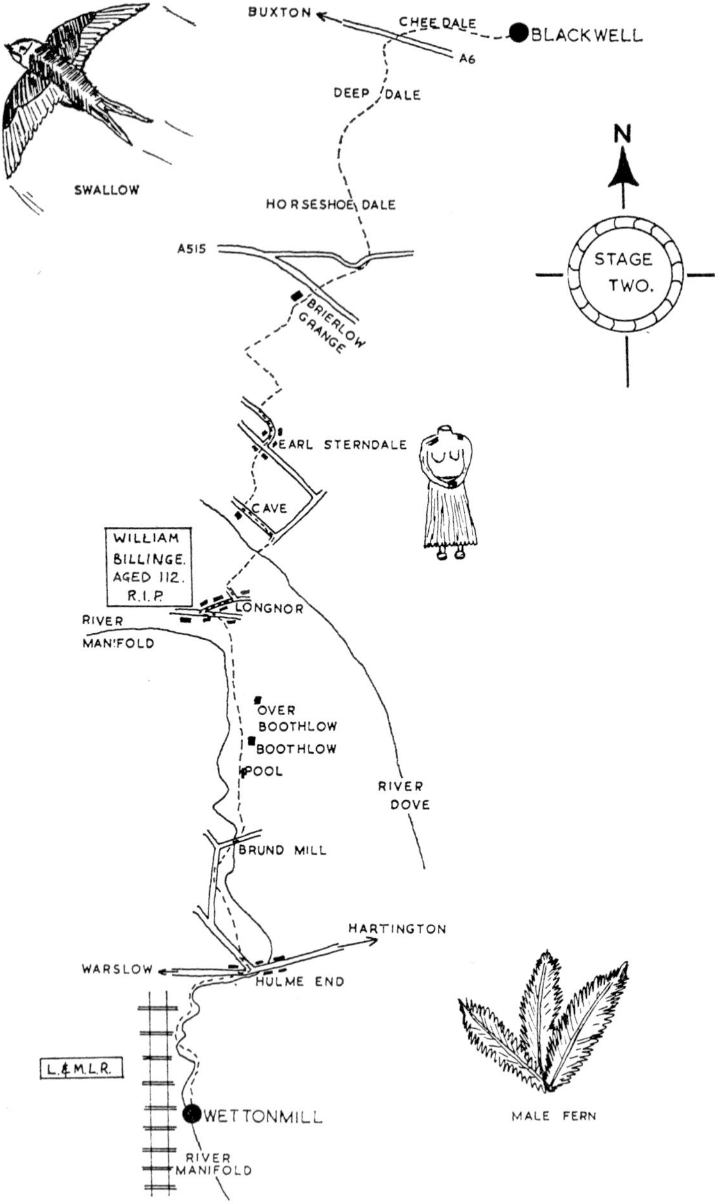
BUXTON
CHEE DALE
BLACKWELL
A6
DEEP DALE
SWALLOW
N
HORSESHOE DALE
A515
STAGE TWO.
BRIERLOW GRANGE
EARL STERNDALE
CAVE
WILLIAM BILLINGE. AGED 112. R.I.P.
LONGNOR
RIVER MANIFOLD
OVER BOOTHLOW
BOOTHLOW
POOL
RIVER DOVE
BRUND MILL
HARTINGTON
WARSLOW
HULME END
L.&M.L.R.
WETTONMILL
MALE FERN
RIVER MANIFOLD

Stage Two: Wettonmill to Blackwell

Route:—	*Wettonmill — Ecton — Hulme End — Hulme House — Brund Mill — Pool — Over Boothlow — Longnor — Cave — Earl Sterndale — Brierlow Grange — Horseshoe Dale — Deep Dale — Chee Dale — Blackwell.*
Distance:—	15 *miles.*
$2\frac{1}{2}$*-inch O.S. Maps:—*	*Sheet Nos. SK* 05, *SK* 06, *SK* 07, *and SK* 17.

AHEAD of you on Stage Two is a fair walk through varied terrain with distant views and quiet beautiful limestone dales. Shouldering your rucksack again, cross the river Manifold via the bridge at Wettonmill. Turn left and, on approaching the farm just round the corner, turn left again along the single track road which weaves its way on the right-hand side of the valley to Swainsley. You can walk along the road on the left-hand side of the valley, which is the line of the old railway, but you meet traffic and have a tunnel to walk through. Just over a mile later you reach the road at Swainsley, where turn left and cross the bridge over the river. At the other side turn right and follow the tarmacadamed path along the line of the Leek and Manifold Railway.

Opposite you as you walk along the old line to Ecton is Ecton Hill, 1,212 ft. high. In this vicinity were the Ecton Copper Mines. They are known to have been mined in the early 17th century and in 1670 gunpowder was used here for the first time in Britain in a mine. The work was only sporadic and little profit was made. In 1739 a Cornish miner found some ore samples while walking on the hill and appreciated what the ground could contain. Permission to mine was granted by the Duke of Devonshire who owned the mining rights. The Cornishmen made several attempts but found little and eventually they sold out at a loss. The next miners dug deeper and found rich deposits which they continued to work until their lease expired after 25 years. The Duke now took over the operation and made the mine a very profitable enterprise—in the 1760s it was annually recording a profit of £10,000. It is reputed that the proceeds from this mine, which contains 15 per cent copper ore, financed the building of that perfect curved building, the Crescent, in Buxton. At the end of the 19th century production ceased—in 1871 it is recorded that only one ton was extracted and twenty years later the mine was abandoned.

On meeting the minor road from Ecton to Warslow, cross over and after a further mile you reach the remains and terminal point of the railway line at Hulme End. At the road, B5054, turn right and then left soon afterwards beside a chapel built in 1834. Follow this minor road for a quarter of a mile. You pass a gate on your right and then the hedge recedes to about three feet high. Here, and you will have to look for it, is the wooden stile which indicates the path going diagonally left across the field to a gritstone stile. This is infrequently walked but all the stiles are there so you shouldn't lose your way. A little over half a mile later you emerge onto another minor road, via a stone stile. Turn right and follow the road for just over a quarter of a mile to Hulme House. Here on its left-hand side is the stile and faint footpath across the field to the road and bridge over the river Manifold. Turn right and cross the bridge.

At the other side you can see the sorrowful shell of Brund Mill, used originally as a cornmill in 1760. Thirty years later Thomas Cantrell and his three sons used it for cotton spinning and calico making, but they ran into financial difficulties and had to sell four years later. For a while it served as a saw mill and during the last war it was used for grinding corn. Much of the machinery still remains inside and, as at the mill near the gates to Okeover Hall, the waterwheel is inside the building and not on one of the walls as is usual.

Walk past the mill and past two other partially collapsed buildings, and at the "Y"-junction of the roads you will see a stone stile on your left. Ascend this and for two miles you will cross the fields to reach Longnor whose cluster of buildings hugs the upper slopes of the valley ahead of you. The stiles will guide you all the way and only the faint line of a path is discernible in places. First you cross the fields and walk past a bend in the river Manifold before cutting across other fields to the next bend. Here you leave the river and traverse other fields to the farm at Pool. Keep to the left of it and descend to a small stream which has a footbridge over it. Soon afterwards you cross a walled grass lane and then traverse further fields, passing the farms of Boothlow and Over Boothlow well on your right. A mile from the walled lane you walk beside the Manifold for a short distance before turning right, ascending to a farm and entering Longnor village.

The stretch between Brund Mill and Longnor is delightful walking. In summer the farmers are all busy cutting the grass, turning it over, baling it or taking it to the barn. It is a busy scene and one that makes one proud to be alive and be an Englishman. The flowers too are a rich variety. At Brund Mill are a large number of the blue nettled-leaved bellflower. The smaller blue harebells around, and great willow herb, dandelions, knapweed, clover, male fern, foxgloves, cow parsley and ragged robin are some of the other flowers you will see. Incidentally, if you are superstitious, you should not pick the pink ragged robins for they bring you bad luck. Birds too are plentiful with swallows flitting about and sitting on the telephone wires. Thrush, rook, linnet, snipe, curlew and blue tits all add their song. On the river you will often see or disturb a moorhen.

On gaining the village of Longnor you are over half way through the day's alloted task so have a rest. There are one or two things to have a look at and there is also a pub here. On reaching the High Street turn left to the Market Square. High on the walls of the Market Hall, which was built in 1873, is a table of tolls payable at Longnor markets and fairs. It is dated 1903 and has lists for buyers and sellers. An example for sellers is; "For every basket of Eggs or other articles for sale . . . One penny", and for buyers, "For every Cow or Bull two years old . . . . Two pence."

While you are sitting in Longnor resting what I hope are not too weary limbs, you are at the point where the Dove and Manifold valleys come nearest together. You are also at the end of the Manifold section of the Way. Years ago the villagers of Longnor made it an annual event to springclean their houses. Everyone in the village would on the appointed day go right through the house and never a bit of dust would be found afterwards. Often the more tired or lazy persons left their brushes and mops outside that night. During the small hours the fairies would come and remove their tools and place them on Sheen Hill, two and a half miles away. In the morning the lazy ones would see their loss and have to walk over to the hill to collect their tools. Often they complained to the authorities but to no avail, and besides they knew who the "fairies" were.

Leave the Market Square by Chapel Street which will bring you to the gates of the church, built in 1780 and of classical design. The outside portrays two storeys but inside the upper is hidden by a false ceiling. The graveyard has many epitaphs and down in the right-hand corner is the gravestone to William Billinge, who died on 25th January 1791 at nearby Fawfieldhead at the age of 112. The gravestone, which is a copy of the original, was placed here in 1903. Billinge was born in a cornfield at Fawfieldhead in 1679 and led an adventurous life in the army serving under the Duke of Marlborough at the Battle of Ramillies on 23rd May 1706. He was at the siege of Gibraltar, Ostend, Lisle, Tournay, Mens, Bethune, Air St. Venant and Bonchain. Only once was he wounded, while rescuing the Duke of Marlborough. A musket shot lodged in his thigh and thirty years afterwards it worked its way to the surface and he removed it, calling it his "French Cherry." He was also involved in the suppression of the Stewart rebellions of 1712 and 1745. Alas, his original epitaph is not included on his new gravestone, but here it is:

Conquests I shared in many a dreadful scene,
With Matchless Marlboro and with brave Eugene.
To peaceful quarters billeted am I,
And here forgetful of my labours lie.
Let me alone awhile, asleep, not slain,
And when the trumpet sounds I'll march again.

From Longnor church turn right along the road and, instead of descending to the main road in the village, bear left further ahead. On reaching a black tarred wooden building on your left beside another road, turn left and at the "T" junction at the top turn left again and then first right along a rough descending track. Before you descend, stand on the brink of the hill and enjoy the extensive view. Below is the infant Dove, in front is Hitter Hill which you will be climbing shortly and to your left are the interesting hills of Parkhouse and Chrome which are limestone reef knolls. This area is particularly good for finding fossils as it is carboniferous limestone and was once the sea bed. Descend the track and where it turns right to the sewage works keep straight ahead and ascend the rise. Over the top is the river Dove and a footbridge across it. Notice as you cross the river that the fields you have been walking through have had gritstone walls and the fields after the river all have limestone walls.

From the bridge you have a wide walled grass track to follow. As you stride out both grey and pied wagtails skip about close by and the swift wall hopper, the wren, plays hide and seek behind the limestone stones. On reaching the road at the top turn left and follow it for half a mile past the farms of Underhill and Cave. At Cave you will see the footpath sign indicating the path on your right to Earl Sterndale. This is your first piece of climbing on the Way; it is short and a good introduction to things to come. First ascend the field before bearing left as you climb close to the summit of Hitter Hill. The stiles are there. Near the summit you descend to the village of Earl Sterndale, aptly entering past the inn named *The Quiet Woman.*

The inn sign depicts a woman minus her head. The story goes that a former landlord visited Longnor market each week and regularly returned at the same time after each visit. On one occasion he was delayed and his wife grew anxious and sent a servant to enquire of his whereabouts. When the landlord did return he was furious at his wife and she was likewise just as annoyed. A row followed and the husband, seeing he was not going to get any sense out of his wife, strode outside and commanded that if he could not have a quiet woman inside he would have one outside and instructed the sign to be painted.

From the inn, cross the road and walk up past the 19th century church. Bear left where the road curves left and a quarter of a mile later pass a small disused quarry on your right. On its left-hand side turn right and ascend the path and steps with a hand rail to guide you. Climb diagonally to your left using the metal posts as guides and just over the brow reach a walled lane. In theory you should go straight across but the quarry activities are now so extensive that the path has been diverted as signposted. The Peak District is extremely rich in mineral wealth, but the quarries are in fact just outside the National Park as the boundary circles this area. Turn left as directed and follow the track for about half a mile. A concrete shelter is provided here for use when blasting is in progress; the blasting times are 9-15 a.m., 12-30 p.m. and 4-15 p.m.

After half a mile you reach another quarry. Here you turn right as directed and begin crossing the fields, all of which have signposts and stiles so that no one should lose their way. This is the only area in Derbyshire where I have seen a red fox during the day. For the better part of half a mile you weave your way through the fields, eventually crossing a now disused railway line. Almost immediately afterwards the signposts point across the fields, indicating the route to Chelmorton. Instead of following them, bear left along a farm track running beside a wood and along the course of another disused railway line. At the end of the wood turn right and walk past Brierlow Grange to the A515 road. Cross the road and on the other side, about thirty yards from the farm drive and hidden in the undergrowth, is the stile. Having located this, cross the field and descend into the upper reaches of Horseshoe Dale, which takes its name from the shape of the valley. Head down to the prominent bend in the road and the stile is on its right-hand side. Cross the minor Chelmorton road and continue down Horseshoe Dale, passing through the small farm at the beginning and then bearing left.

You now begin to walk down one of the quieter and yet more attractive limestone dales of the Peak District. It may not have a river or towering buttresses but these you will see shortly. You are walking along one of the old bridle paths, known as the Priests' Way, which leaves the valley shortly to continue to Buxton. On your left you pass Back Dale before entering one of the loveliest dales, Deep Dale. Soon you round a corner and there stand numerous buttresses and trees creating a captivating scene. Ahead is Thirst House Cave with its 15 ft. high and 20 ft. wide entranceway. To potholers it is a very easy cave and you can crawl along for about 200 ft.

Thirst House Cave has yielded a wide range of archaeological finds. The cave's wealth was first discovered by Mr. Matthew Salt, a tradesman of Buxton, in 1884. Among the many items he found there over the next few years were red deer antlers, bones from sheep, short-horned Celtic ox, horse, fox and hare, the skull of a bear, many fragments of pottery and numerous Roman brooches. Some of these finds can be seen in Buxton Museum. All this indicated that the cave was occupied during the first and second centuries A.D. The flowers around the cave are particularly grand with numerous delicate harebells, field scabious and blood red geraniums.

In the 1800s Deep Dale was a reputed haunt of fairy folk. A tale was still told early this century of a traveller who was walking through the dale when he saw several fairies. Stealthily he reached out and caught one, put it into a sack and set off for home. He had not gone far before the fairy began to scream. It screamed so loudly and constantly that the traveller let it out and continued on his way.

Continue down the dale which in its later stages has a small stream running through it. The end of the valley is a sad sight because of a quarry, and the easiest way round this is by walking down the quarry road to the main A6. The blasting times at the quarry are, Monday to Friday between 4 p.m. and 6 p.m., and Saturday between 12 noon and 4 p.m. The limestone here at Topley Pike is at approximately 2,500 ft. the thickest in the Peak District.

Down at the road the constant stream of cars brings you back to the twentieth century with a vengeance. Cross the A6 and follow the rough track down Chee Dale for half a mile. Opposite the footbridge across the river Wye turn right and ascend to the disused railway, crossing it via the bridge. The line was part of the Midland Railway and linked Bakewell and Buxton, passenger services along it commencing on 1st June 1863. Just over a hundred years later Bakewell was the last station to close on 1st July 1968.

Cross the bridge before ascending to the left-hand side of the small valley and gaining the top of Chee Dale. The view down into it is very impressive with Plum Buttress, 270 feet high and the highest limestone face in Derbyshire, dominating the scene. The stiles are lost around here. Simply head to the left-hand side of a farm building and to its left on the brow of the hill is the walled grass track which you follow all the way to Blackwell. On meeting the village road keep straight ahead and at the bottom is Cross Roads Farm and the camp site. The hamlet of Blackwell is part of Taddington parish. In Taddington church, just over a mile away, are memorials to the Blackwell family who were Lords of the Manor.

That's another stage over and, although you will no doubt be feeling tired, tomorrow is not so bad as you leave the limestone and begin walking through the gritstone country. A change is as good as a rest—so they say.

The author on his inaugural walk of the Peakland Way

Rural tranquility at Wettonmill (Stage One)

The Market Square, Ashbourne (Stage One)

The richly ornamented Ilam Cross (Stage One)

Peak Forest church and its large graveyard (Stage Three)

Kinder Downfall in winter; figures at top left give an idea of its scale (Stage Four)

Stage Three: Blackwell to Barber Booth

Route:-	*Blackwell — Chee Dale — Wormhill — Monksdale House — Wheston — Dale Head — Hay Dale — Dam Dale — Peak Forest — Broctor — Old Moor — Windy Knoll — Mam Tor — Hollins Cross — Barber Booth.*
Distance:-	13 *miles.*
2½*-inch O.S. Maps:-*	*Sheet Nos. SK* 17 *and SK* 18.

On Stage Three you have a magnificent walk in front of you as you leave the limestone country and enter the gritstone. Picturesque dales give way to rugged mountains as you ascend Mam Tor and move to the base of Kinder Scout.

From Blackwell follow the farm track past Hall Green. Beyond here cross the field and at the end turn right and then left immedately afterwards to traverse the fields of the spur of Chee Tor. At the top of Chee Dale you can see the footbridge over the river Wye below and the path beyond bearing left as it climbs to Wormhill. This is a grand viewpoint and you can look down to Miller's Dale on your right. Descend, cross the bridge and ascend to Wormhill.

As you reach Wormhill from Chee Dale, ahead of you can be seen Wormhill Hall. The hall, whose date of building is unknown except that a rainwater head is dated 1697, is owned by one of the most well-known families in Derbyshire, the Bagshawes. Other family seats once included Banner Cross Hall and Oakes Park, both of which are in Sheffield, and Ford Hall near Chapel-en-le-Frith. The latter was the home of William Bagshawe, 1628-1702, an ardent non-conformist who preached all over Derbyshire and earned himself the title "The Apostle of the Peak". His first sermon was preached at Wormhill Chapel in 1649.

The manor of Wormhill was part of the Royal Forest of the Peak, whose borders were the four rivers of Etherow, Derwent, Wye and Goyt. It was once owned by Henry de Ferrers, who was given a total of 114 manors in Derbyshire by William the Conqueror, and then passed through several owners until 1646 when Adam Bagshawe

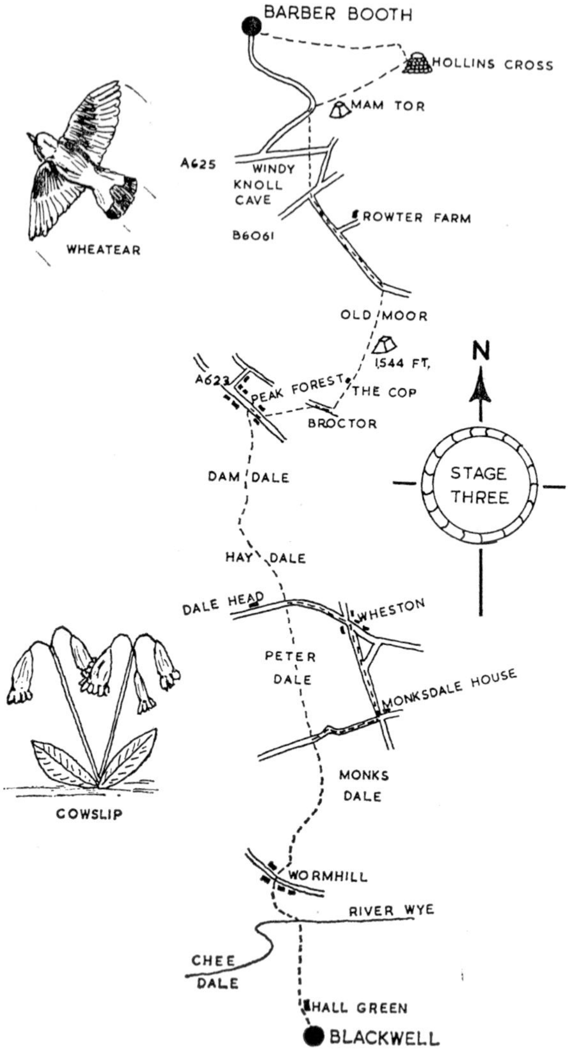
BARBER BOOTH
HOLLINS CROSS
MAM TOR
A625
WINDY
KNOLL
CAVE
ROWTER FARM
B6061
WHEATEAR
OLD MOOR
1544 FT.
N
A623
PEAK FOREST
THE COP
BROCTOR
DAM DALE
STAGE
THREE
HAY DALE
DALE HEAD
WHESTON
PETER
DALE
MONKSDALE HOUSE
COWSLIP
MONKS
DALE
WORMHILL
RIVER WYE
CHEE
DALE
HALL GREEN
BLACKWELL

became the Lord of the Manor. Previous to this, during the Royal Forest years, people living in Wormhill who held tenure of land were called "Wolf Hunters." Wolves abounded in the forest and the last one is reputed to have been killed in 1490.

Turn left at the road in Wormhill and ascend gently to the few houses. Opposite the shop turn right and follow the road to St. Margaret's church. Before you do so, notice on your left a large drinking well erected in 1875 in memory of James Brindley. He was born at Tunstead in the parish of Wormhill in 1716, had no education and even as an adult could hardly write his name. Yet he became one of the most remarkable canal builders of all time, working everything out in his head and never with pen and paper. He constructed 369 miles of canals for the Duke of Bridgwater, including the Manchester and Liverpool and the Trent and Mersey.

St Margaret's church was rebuilt in 1864, but the original chapel —Wormhill was a chapelry of Tideswell—dates from the late 13th century. When Wormhill became an ecclesiastical parish in 1859 it was felt that a larger building was needed. The unusual tower, whose base dates from 1273, is supposed to be a copy of the Saxon tower at Stomping in Sussex. The peal of six bells is reputed to be the smallest in existence. The foundry, J. Taylor & Co. of Loughborough originally cast eight miniature bells as samples of its craft. Six were placed in the church and bear the date 1863; the sixth was found to be faulty and was recast the following year. It is recorded that on the occasion of Ann Brightmore's wedding at Wormhill church, she came direct from Wormhill Hall where she worked still carrying her sweeping brush. Her husband-to-be was busy working on the church roof and he came down at the appointed hour with a trowel in his hand. Despite what appears to have been a hasty marriage, Ann lived happily and died at the age of 103.

A little past the church the lane divides. To the right is the rectory and on your left is a walled path. Walk up this to the end of the walled section, about 20 yards later, and cross the following field by heading for a large hawthorn tree at the top left-hand corner. On the right-hand side of the tree is the stile. Cross this and continue along a walled path, following its curvature as it descends down to the road in between Peter and Monk's Dale. Almost at the road you leave the walled section behind and cross a field. Much of Monk's Dale, which takes its name from the monks of Lenton Priory who had a small grange here, and a small part of Peter Dale are a National Nature Reserve. Officially established on 15th December 1972, Monk's Dales Reserve occupies an area of 35 acres. The main part of what is called "The Derbyshire Dales National Nature Reserve" lies in Lathkill Dale and comprises 123 acres.

There is a footpath through Peter Dale to Dale End which is a right-of-way and links up with the original line of the Peakland Way. Those wishing to by-pass the historical village of Wheston can walk up Peter Dale. It is very picturesque and peaceful, but Wheston does have two interesting curiosities so make up your mind which route to follow.

The "original routers" should turn right and ascend the minor road to the first house on your left, Monksdale House, where turn left and continue along another minor road to Wheston. Half a mile later the road bears right to the village. Keep straight ahead on the rough track to the centre of the village, and here turn left. Immediately on your left is Wheston Hall, which was built by the Charlton family and dates from the 17th and 18th centuries. The hall has been the scene of many ghost stories and the following is just one of them. Once a year a barefoot lady clad in a nightgown walks three times round the house. As she does so she shrieks at the top of her voice and pulls at her long golden hair. She married a man she never loved and her true lover retired to Wheston Hall to mourn his loss. His neighbours said his only friend was the Devil. One day his lover escaped from her husband and came to the hall. It wasn't long before her husband found her but he is believed to have been murdered for he was never seen again. His wife died at the hall later and is buried in Tideswell graveyard. For penance for the crime committed she makes the annual pilgrimage to the hall.

Just after the hall you pass on your left Wheston Cross. Originally it stood outside the hall but when this was rebuilt it was moved to its present position. This wayside cross, the finest in Derbyshire, dates from the 15th century and stands 11½ feet high. The upper part of the cross portrays on one side the baby Christ in the arms of Mary, his mother, while the other side illustrates Christ on the cross at Calvary. Continue down the road until in the bottom you near the house of Dale End—on your left are the rocky limestone buttresses of Peter Dale. Turn right and walk along the bottom of Hay Dale, which in its upper reaches is particularly attractive as you pass through a thinly populated wood.

Emerging from the stile at the top of the dale, bear right and follow the track for a short distance before turning left along the stiled path on the right-hand side of Dam Dale. Keep to this side as you pass close to a farm after a little over half a mile, and half a mile later you reach the main A623 road at Peak Forest. You are more than halfway through the walk and about to leave the limestone country, so take a break and have a look at some of the interesting features of Peak Forest.

It is fitting that many of the historical features of this stage of the walk have been centred on love and marriage. Peak Forest did not come under the jurisdiction of any Bishop, and hence the local vicar had the right to grant probate to wills and issue marriage licences without banns. Between the years 1728 and 1754 Peak Forest became the Gretna Green of Derbyshire. Here anyone could come, at any time of the day or night, and ask to be married immediately. This the vicar would do after the fee was paid and the marriages were then confirmed by his own certificate and seal, both of which are still in existence today. A faithful record was kept by the vicar of these marriages in a book which has become known as the "Foreign Marriage Register." This happy state of affairs ceased when Lord Hardwick's Law was implemented on 25th March 1754, but up to then about one hunded people a year were married in this way. Even today it is possible to be married at Peak Forest without banns during the day, provided that one of the couple live in the village for fifteen days prior to the ceremony.

The place where these runaway marriages took place was dismantled when the present church was built in 1880. The reading room on the right of the church bears the date 1880 and is constructed from the stone of the original chapel, built by the Earl of Devonshire's wife in 1657. Among the gravestones of the churchyard can be seen the stone base and stump of the chapel's font—the font bowl is now in the new church.

If you have had enough rest, turn right and walk through the village of Peak Forest to its outskirts. Here on your left is the stone stile and the path which bears slightly to your right and gently ascends the fields to the road near Broctor. In the spring the fields near the road are full of cowslips. Do by all means look at and admire these delightful yellow flowers, but please don't pick them. At the road turn right to walk past Broctor Farm and then turn left and ascend the road to the farm known as The Cop. Here, as signposted, turn right through the gate and then left immediately afterwards. Climb the walled path, which you soon lose as you ascend the rise close to the triangulation pillar at a height of 1,544 feet on your right. Once over the top you can see ahead the prominent shape of Mam Tor; when this is climbed it is all downhill to Barber Booth. It is magnificent walking now as you approach Old Moor with the gritstone country ahead, limestone all around you and Conies Dale on your left. The beautiful singer and aero-acrobat, the skylark, is heard above you, while along the limestone walls the ubiquitous wren pops up unsuspectedly and the distinct white rump of the wheatear dances along in front of you.

On reaching the rough track on Old Moor, turn left and follow it past Rowter Farm to the minor road, B6061. Go directly across and along the grass track beyond so as to reach the A625 road. Notice that all the walls up to this road are constructed of limestone but beyond it they are gritstone. Just before the A625, on your right, is the limestone cave known as Windy Knoll. This was once the watering place for migratory animals and when it was archaeologically excavated in 1875 some 6,800 bones and 500 teeth were found. All were from the Great Ice Age period of evolution and they included bones from the grizzly bear, reindeer, bison, wolf and sabre-toothed tiger.

At the A625 go straight across, follow the path directly opposite and ascend to the road at the pass between Rushup Edge and Mam Tor. On gaining the road turn right and climb to the summit of Mam Tor, 1,696 feet high. Once there feast your eyes to your left. Below is the Edale Valley with Edale sitting snugly at the start of Grindsbrook; further left is Barber Booth at the end of the walk; and beyond that towers Kinder, the highest part of the Peak District and the hardest part of the whole Way. To your right is the Hope Valley and the villages of Castleton, Hope and Hathersage located on the valley floor. In the far distance is Win Hill, yet another mountain to climb in two days time.

Around the summit plateau of Mam Tor is a single rampart ditch, about seven feet deep, which is all that you can see of an Iron Age fort that existed here. The fort has been excavated several times and finds include a polished stone axe, a Bronze Age socketed axe, parts of a shale bracelet and fragments of pottery. From the summit continue down the ridge, which I nickname the "Peakland Ridge," to the memorial cairn at Hollins Cross to John Hyett, a founder member of the Long Eaton Rambling Club. Here turn left and begin descending towards Barber Booth. After approximately 200 yards bear left again, following a wide track and then a footpath to the farm road just to the right of Greenlands. Continue down the track to the first bend and there on your left is the stone stile. Ascend this and cross the fields and several streams via footbridges to the road at Barber Booth.

The camp site at Waterside Farm is a quarter of a mile away on the Edale road to your right. That completes your third day of the walk. By now blisters will have appeared and muscles will be complaining, but you will be feeling fitter, looking about you more and possibly even enjoying the walk. Now's the time to relax and lie in front of your tent with the sun bronzing your face to the envy of your friends. How delicious food tastes outside—the soup, the stew, the fruit and coffee all have a magical taste that you never capture at home. Perhaps it is the pieces of grass which always find their way onto your spoon!

Stage Four: Barber Booth to Hagg Farm

Route:-	*Barber Booth — Upper Booth — Jacob's Ladder — Kinder Low* (2,077 *ft.*) *— Kinder Downfall — Ashop Head — Snake Path — Snake Inn — Course of Roman Road — Hayridge Farm — Roman Road — Rowlee Bridge — Rowlee Farm — Hagg Farm.*
Distance:-	13 *miles.*
$2\frac{1}{2}$*-inch O.S. Map:-*	*Outdoor Leisure Map, "The Dark Peak."*

YOU have now had three days of continuous walking and your muscles will be becoming accustomed to the task, your rucksack won't feel as heavy and you will—I hope—be bouncing with energy. You need to be, for today's section is the toughest and the most challenging of the Way and one that you will derive endless pleasure from doing.

Retrace your steps back to the bridge over the river Noe, where turn right and walk into the hamlet of Barber Booth. Take the second road on your left in the hamlet and walk past the houses and farm before crossing the railway line. After the bridge turn sharp left, and 200 yards later turn right and follow the gritstone stiled footpath all the way to the hamlet of Upper Booth. Ahead loom the ramparts of Kinder. At Upper Booth turn left through the hamlet, and at the road go to the right and begin the walk above the river Noe to the footbridge at the base of Jacob's Ladder. First you follow a tarmacadamed lane and then a rough track.

Having crossed the bridge engage into low gear and gradually ascend Jacob's Ladder. The secret of climbing this, as with all mountains, is to keep a slow steady pace having as few stops as possible, otherwise you will disrupt your rhythm and breathing. You will be surprised, by using this method, how soon you have ascended the steep section. Above it you have a gentle climb up a rough wide path. On reaching the base of the hill, Swine's Back, turn sharp right and ascend the path which skirts the right-hand side of the hill's summit. Once here you are in the realm of peat and the climbing is all but over. From the hill head for the gritstone

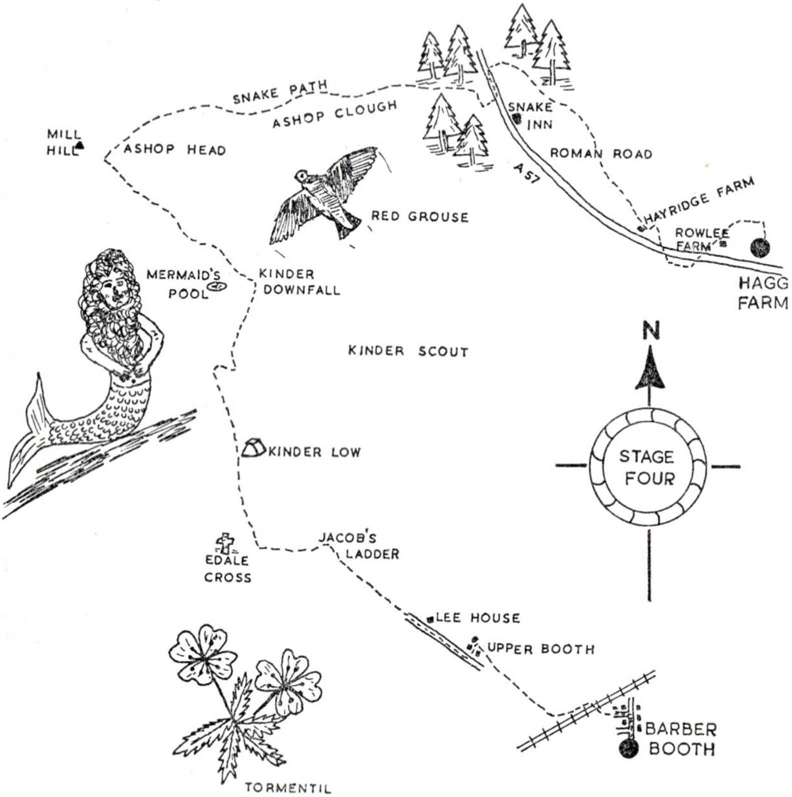
SNAKE PATH
ASHOP CLOUGH
MILL HILL
ASHOP HEAD
SNAKE INN
ROMAN ROAD
A57
HAYRIDGE FARM
ROWLEE FARM
HAGG FARM
RED GROUSE
MERMAID'S POOL
KINDER DOWNFALL
KINDER SCOUT
N
STAGE FOUR
KINDER LOW
JACOB'S LADDER
EDALE CROSS
LEE HOUSE
UPPER BOOTH
BARBER BOOTH
TORMENTIL

outcrop, Edale Rocks, before continuing past the triangulation pillar on Kinder Low (2,077 ft.). Keep straight ahead, heading for the rim of the plateau where there is a well-trodden path which will take you to Kinder Downfall. Because the surface is peat, which makes path identification awkward, you are well advised to use a compass from Swine's Back to Kinder Low and then to the Downfall. In mist a compass here is of paramount importance.

The moorland of Kinder and Bleaklow is privately owned. Walkers have been crossing this terrain for many years and in the first half of this century they were trespassing. In 1932 hundreds of walkers took part in a mass trespass walk on Kinder, but today it is a completely different story. Following the National Parks Act of 1949, access agreements between the Peak Park Planning Board and the moor owners secured permission for walkers to cross the moors. During the grouse shooting season from the glorious twelfth of August until 10th December each year, certain areas of moorland are closed to the public on specific days. At access points to the moors, such as the way you came at Jacob's Ladder, notices and maps are posted indicating which area is closed and when.

How do you like walking across this black slippery surface? In the summer it can be exasperating work, but in the winter it freezes and makes a good walking surface. The peat you are crossing is very thick and biologists have taken samples of it from different levels. From the pollen grains in the peat it has been possible to build up a picture of the vegetation of the area. Peat is formed from dead plants which accumulate in waterlogged areas and attain thick layers as no bacterial activity takes place to reduce the plant remains. Some 11,000 years ago, following the last ice age, only trees such as willows, juniper and rowan grew. A thousand years later the climate became warmer and birch and pine were growing, while 800 years later in 7,600 B.C. oak, elm and hazel trees were flourishing. In 5,600 B.C. the climate was warm but wet and the formation began of the peat we see today, which is basically Sphagnum moss. The drainage channels, which are locally called groughs, began to form in the peat from about 600 B.C. when the climate was similar to that of today. The present covering of heather, bilberry and cotton grass has been created by man who has both drained and burnt the area. Charcoal has been found in the peat, and by carbon methods has been dated at 1,300 A.D. Sphagnum moss was used extensively in hospitals during World War One as a surgical dressing because of its absorbent qualities.

As you are walking along the edge of the Kinder plateau, Kinder Reservoir and Hayfield are down on your left. Before you reach Kinder Downfall you will more than likely flush out a red grouse, which will utter its startled cry and fly low and intermittently over the ground. This truly native British bird lives almost entirely on ling heather which carpets much of Kinder. During April and May the female makes a small hollow in the ground which she lines with grass or heather to make her nest. She may have between four and nine eggs, which are creamy white in colour and covered with dark brown blotches. You may also startle a mountain or blue hare; this animal changes its fur colour to white in winter and is often very conspicuous against the dark background when no snow has fallen. It is named the blue hare because in the spring and autumn when it is changing coats the white and brown fur together give a bluish appearance.

Ahead you will see the dramatic valley sides strewn with boulders and large gritstone rock faces and, ascending to the edge, will be confronted by the spectacular sight of Kinder Downfall. Here a thin stream weaves its way over part of Kinder before tumbling down 100 feet and continuing its way into Kinder Reservoir. The scene is captivating whatever the weather or season. If a westerly wind is blowing the downfall becomes an upfall as the water is thrown back onto the plateau. But there is only one time to see the fall in all its glittering glory and that is in winter. Then the fall and surrounding area are covered with thousands of shimmering icicles creating a scene of unfathomed splendour.

While admiring the grandeur of the scene, this is a good place to halt, rest your limbs, savour the view and eat your orange. No doubt my name was mud as you toiled up Jacob's Ladder but now you can see why. Wasn't it worth it? While you are eating your segments here is a legend for you to ponder over. Part way down the valley on the right-hand side of the river is a small pool known as the "Mermaid's Pool." The story goes that each Easter Eve a mermaid can be seen here at midnight. For those who see her, immortality is the prize:

Just when the early dawn broke o'er the hills,
And shed grey twilight o'er the gloomy vales,
The Mermaid might be seen . . . . . .
Woman, and fish, so strangely blent in one . . . . . .
Now on the velvet bank in sportive play;
Into long flowing locks it curl'd its hair,
Breathes the swift zephyrs as they rise,
And its fair bosom heaves with human sighs;
But when the fish prevails beneath the tides,
Like lightening it a scaly monster glides;
And in its wat'ry cavern must remain
Till Easter Sunday morning comes again.

(Taken from H. Redfern's poem—"*The Mermaid Pool, Kinder.*")

Few if any have seen her, but the people of Hayfield firmly believed in the legend up to 150 years ago. One of the local characters, Aaron Ashton, regularly came to the pool, each year, but no one knows whether he actually saw the mermaid. Perhaps he did, for he died aged 104 in 1835.

Having set you into good spirits and banished all thoughts of tiredness, cross the top of the Downfall and continue round the perimeter of Kinder Scout. You are now following a small section of Britain's longest long-distance path, The Pennine Way, your course up here via Upper Booth being one of the alternative routes on this Way. Continue round the edge as you go along a wide path, heading in a north-west direction. At the north-west corner of the plateau you descend to Ashop Head, where you leave the Pennine Way and turn right to begin descending the Snake Path down Ashop Clough. Once here you know the worst is over and for approximately three miles you descend with a brook on your right. In the later stages you walk through part of the Snake Plantation and cross the river Ashop via a footbridge before ascending to the Snake road, A57.

If you are seeking refreshment there is the *Snake Inn* on your right 200 yards away. Purists should turn left and after 200 yards turn right on to the footpath along the course of an old Roman road. You follow this for the next three miles almost to the end of today's walk. The path first passes through part of the Snake Plantation before running close to it and descending into Oyster Clough. The Roman road is known as Doctor's Gate but to walkers it is the "High Street of the Peak"—it is a remarkable viewpoint with Kinder on your right and the Woodlands Valley in front.

As to how the road became named "Doctor's Gate," remains a mystery. The only shred of evidence is the following local legend concerning a very clever magician who has been termed a local Dr. Faust. The doctor called the Devil and challenged him to a race. Although surprised at the Doctor's challenge, for all knew the Devil had the fastest steed ever groomed, he agreed. At length the terms were settled. The doctor was to be allowed a good start, and should he win he was to have his freedom. If the doctor lost, the Devil stipulated:-

On a day which I shall name, thou shalt wait upon me
and deliver up thy soul to me.

The doctor could only agree. The course of the race was the line of the Roman road, and the Devil allowed the doctor a good start —in fact more than he had planned to for he was feeling over-confident. When the doctor was nearly on the skyline, the Devil set off at an alarming speed. In no time he was approaching the doctor who, seeing the Devil catch him up, pressed his horse harder. The Devil, feeling like having some fun, reached out and twisted the tail of the doctor's horse. The aim was to make the horse squeal and lose speed, but instead it had the opposite effect and the horse galloped faster. While this foolery was carrying on, the Devil was unaware of the approaching stream. At the last second he realised his mistake and tugged at the horse's tail to make the animal stop. But it was too late and the doctor and the Devil crossed the water. The Devil naturally abided by the laws of sorcery, one of which is that when a pursued person crosses water the power of evil has no command over him. Thus the Devil retired hurt and ashamed at being beaten, and the doctor returned triumphant and lived happily for many years.

The Roman road appears to have been built about 78 A.D. and links the two Roman forts of Brough (Navio) near Bradwell with the Glossop camp known as Melandra. Where it passes the summit of Snake Pass at 1,654 feet, the road has been uncovered and is 10 ft. wide—6 ft. of road with 2 ft. either side for ditches. From Oyster Clough you curve round the hillside keeping a gritstone wall on your right, and soon you begin to descend gradually and follow a track as you near Hayridge Farm. Here you turn left and follow the farm track towards Alport Farm. About 250 yards up this you turn right and follow the path through the trees to Alport Bridge.

Cross the A57 and descend to the river which you go over via the wooden footbridge. Afterwards bear left and continue along the path on the course of the Roman road to the left of Upper Ashop Farm. A little past the farm the tracks divide; here you turn left and descend to the river which you cross via Rowlee Bridge and then follow the surfaced lane to the A57. Cross over and walk past Rowlee Farm, and take the zig-zagged track beyond. It soon levels out and you pass Bellhagg Barn on your right. Shortly afterwards you come to a cross-roads of bridle paths, where you turn right and descend down to Hagg Farm and the camp site.

The end of the day's walk is reached. Here is a small shop and water, and you have the use of the hostel's common room and drying room. You are now over half way round the Peakland Way, and this makes a fitting stopping place to sort out your gear, wash and relax in company. It is pleasant to relax, and recount the Way so far and the day's walk in particular. Tomorrow's route takes you from the moorland country into the gritstone edges, and four days from now and you will be back in Ashbourne.

Stage Five: Hagg Farm to Hathersage

Route:-	*Hagg Farm — Hope Cross — Roman Road — Win Hill — Thornhill — Shatton — River Derwent — Hathersage*
Distance:-	11 *miles.*
$2\frac{1}{2}$*-inch O.S. Maps:-*	*Sheet Nos. SK* 18 *and SK*28.

THIS is the lazy day of the Way, even though we climb Win Hill. From Hagg Farm go down the tarmacadamed lane to the A57 road, and go straight across to the wooden gate and continue descending down a track in a wooded hollow. On reaching the river Ashop, cross it via the Haggwater Bridge, immediately after turning left to follow the grass track. Just after passing the farm buildings of Hagglee on your left, turn right and follow the zig-zag grass track through the trees. Leaving them behind you walk beside the forest before gaining the ridge crest. As you ascend to it, the grandeur of the scene unfolds with the wooded valley below and Ladybower Reservoir becoming more and more dominate. Sparrowhawks quarter the ground above you and the dainty harebells litter the trackside. At the crest turn left and follow the track on the course of the Roman road, an earlier part of which you covered late yesterday.

You descend first of all to Hope Cross, which bears the date 1737 but is reputed to be older. During the days of packhorse travel this was one of the signposts, and on the four sides can be seen the place names of Hope, Sheffield, Glossop and Edale. From the cross keep straight ahead to follow the wide track and head for the summit of Win Hill. The track soon descends towards Hope, but you keep straight ahead and about a mile and a half later you reach the summit of Win Hill, 1,518 feet. It is a squat but imposing peak with a small rocky ridge leading to the top.

As I said this is a lazy day, so drop your rucksack and absorb the view for it is very extensive. To your right is the Hope Valley with the villages of Hope and Bamford. Beyond that is Offerton Moor and behind you is Castleton and Mam Tor, which you climbed two

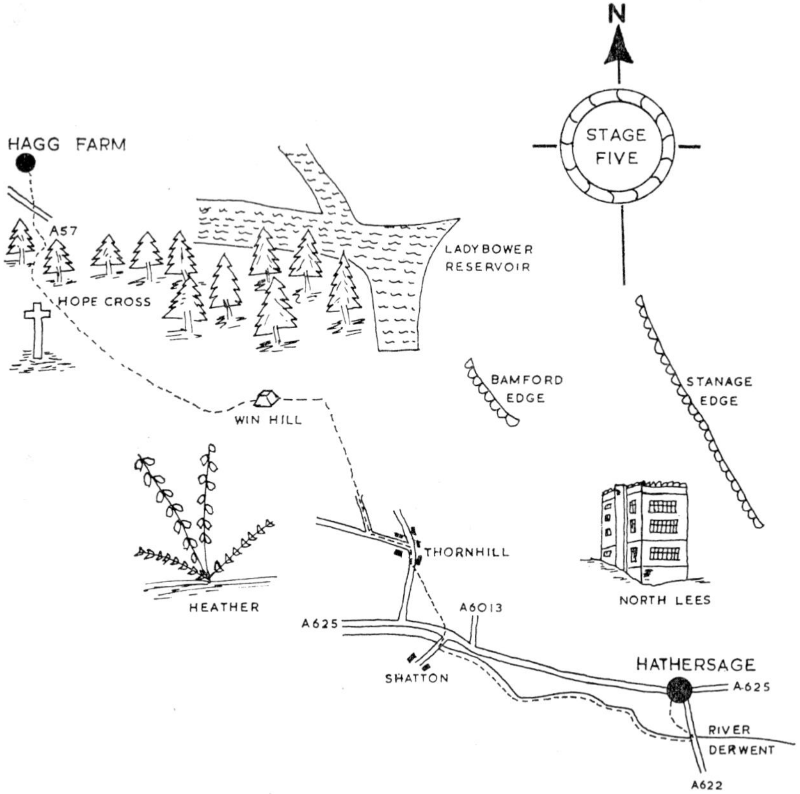
N
STAGE FIVE
HAGG FARM
A57
HOPE CROSS
LADYBOWER RESERVOIR
BAMFORD EDGE
STANAGE EDGE
WIN HILL
HEATHER
THORNHILL
NORTH LEES
A6013
A625
SHATTON
HATHERSAGE
A625
RIVER DERWENT
A622

days ago. Below you are extensive woodlands, Ladybower Reservoir and its two legs, and the Derwent Moors beyond. Ladybower Reservoir is the third reservoir of a chain of three—the other two, Howden and Derwent, were built at the beginning of this century. Ladybower was started in 1935, completed ten years later and officially opened by King George the Sixth on 25th September, 1945. During the ten years of building, 100,000 tons of clay and 1,000,000 tons of earth were moved. The depth of the reservoir reaches a maximum of 135 feet, it covers a surface area of 504 acres and holds a total capacity of 6,300 million gallons. The water is used by Derby, Leicester, Nottingham and Sheffield. Lying underneath the water level are two villages, Ashopton and Derwent. During exceptionally dry periods the reservoir level drops and the ruins of Derwent village are seen. The last time this happened was in 1969.

Across the valley is Lose Hill. According to a local tradition there was a battle here in the 7th century when the winners occupied Win Hill and the losers occupied Lose Hill. Following the attempted assassination of Edwin, King of Northumbria, in approximately 630 A.D., Edwin marched with his army to battle with his would-be assassins, Cynegils and Cuichelm, the Kings of Wessex. Edwin was on the scene first and placed his men on the highest hill, Win Hill. Cynegils and Cuichelm arrived later and were joined by Penda, the King of Mercia. The following day the battle raged and, although the Kings of Wessex had a much larger army, Edwin skilfully destroyed many of their warriors forcing them to beat a hurried retreat home. Edwin lost half his army in the conflict but arrived home in triumph.

From the summit descend by heading towards Bamford Edge, first crossing a wooden ladder stile over a gritstone wall before walking through a thin plantation. On reaching the fence of the main plantation turn right and continue on the wide path along the eastern perimeter of Win Hill, overlooking Bamford. Just over half a mile later you begin the gradual descent towards Thornhill. In front of you is the magnificent view of the Hope Valley with Hathersage, your destination, at its head. A quarter of a mile from Thornhill you merge into a grass lane and descend to the road on the western outskirts of the village. At the road junction turn left into this picturesque and quiet settlement which has neither pub nor post office.

Turn right at the "T"-junction and, on reaching the last house on your left, the footpath for Shatton is on its right-hand side. The path is clear, and a quarter of a mile later you reach the Derwent Water Board Offices. Just in front of them, and on the right-hand side of the wooden gate, is the stile. Continue descending, keeping the hedge on your right, and at the railway embankment bear left. In a few yards you reach the tunnel which you pass through and then walk on the right of the High Peak Garden Centre to the main road, A625. Cross the road and follow the minor road for Shatton—once over the bridge across the Derwent, the stile can be seen on your left. Go through this and begin the most enjoyable 2½ mile walk along the right bank of the river Derwent towards Hathersage.

This is delightful walking with the wide swirling river flowing beside you. Those masterpieces of river country, the dippers, are in profusion here. You will identify them by their white breasts and their bobbing motion on either tree or boulder. Occasionally you will see them working their way upstream as they search for food. Their bodies are so designed that the pressure of water pushes their beaks to the bottom. The occasional water vole will be spotted and many wrens will be seen flitting along the bank side. In the winter months I have seen as many as a dozen grey herons in this area.

Two and a half miles along here and you reach the main road, A622. Turn left, cross the bridge and go through the stile on your left and follow the footpath to the southern edge of Hathersage. Here you join a lane which by keeping straight ahead brings you into the centre of Hathersage; the youth hostel is almost opposite. If you are not feeling too lazy I suggest a visit to Hathersage's church will be a reward for your day's labour. Part of the church dates back to the 12th century but it is largely 14th and 15th century. Before going inside, the main feature to see in the graveyard is Little John's tomb. He is said to have been born in Hathersage and, having buried Robin Hood at Kirklees Priory, he reputedly returned to his native village to die. The tomb is 13½ feet long, and when it was excavated in 1784 a thigh bone 29½ inches long was found. Until approximately the mid-17th century, Little John's cap and bow used to hang in the church. Before going into the building notice the many amusing and gruesome gargoyles. The main interest inside is the Eyre brasses of the 15th century—they are some of the best to be seen in Derbyshire.

The Eyre family has for centuries been associated with the Hope Valley. According to the legend, a person named Truelove fought with William the Conqueror at the battle of Hastings in 1066. During the battle, it is said, William was knocked off his horse and the helmet he wore became crushed and restricted his breathing. Truelove saw what had happened and quickly went to William's aid. He removed the helmet, whereupon William enquired his name. Learning it was Truelove, William said, "From now on your name will be Air for you have given me air to breathe." Later on in the battle William went to see how Air was doing and found he had sustained injuries which resulted in his leg being amputated. William told him that when he was better he would give him some land. Air told him he would call it Hope, for William had given him hope to live. Hence the name of the village and valley! On the

Typical gritstone stile on the Peakland Way (Stage Four)

The plain stump of Hope Cross (Stage Five)

Curbar Edge, characteristic of Derbyshire gritstone country (Stage Six)

Queen Mary's Bower at Chatsworth House (Stage Seven)

Parwich, a village surrounded by rolling hills (Stage Eight)

Gratton Dale, a typical limestone valley (Stage Eight)

High Peak Trail notice-board, showing the symbol of the Peak District National Park (Stage Eight)

brasses you will see the Eyre coat of arms and, as if to add weight to the legend, you will see a single leg above the shield. The Eyre family owned many halls in the area, notably North Lees Hall which you pass tomorrow.

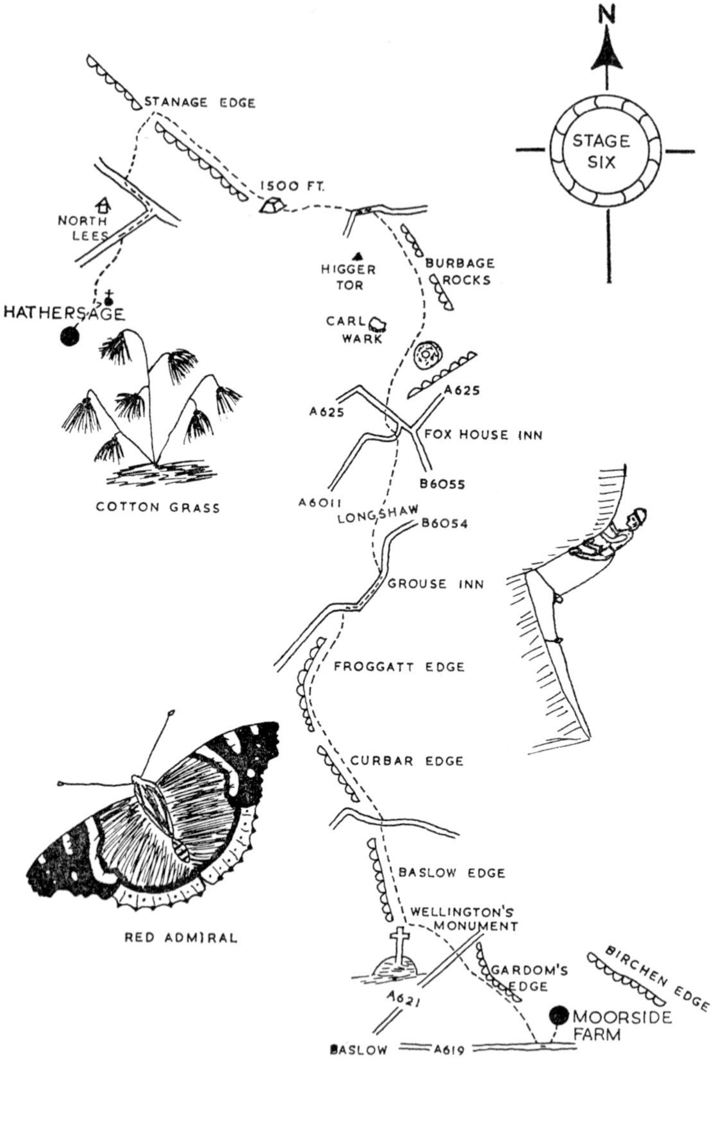
STANAGE EDGE
STAGE SIX
N
1500 FT.
NORTH LEES
HIGGER TOR
BURBAGE ROCKS
HATHERSAGE
CARL WARK
A625
A625
FOX HOUSE INN
B6055
COTTON GRASS
A6011
LONGSHAW
B6054
GROUSE INN
FROGGATT EDGE
CURBAR EDGE
BASLOW EDGE
RED ADMIRAL
WELLINGTON'S MONUMENT
GARDOM'S EDGE
BIRCHEN EDGE
A621
MOORSIDE FARM
BASLOW
A619

Stage Six: Hathersage to Moorside Farm

Route:-	*Hathersage — Stanage Plantation — Stanage Edge — Cowper Stone — Burbage Rocks — Longshaw Lodge — Sheffield Plantation — Grouse Inn — Froggatt Edge — Curbar Edge — Baslow Edge — Wellington's Monument — Gardom's Edge — Moorside Farm.*
Distance:-	$12\frac{1}{2}$ *miles.*
$2\frac{1}{2}$*-inch O.S. Maps:-*	*Sheet Nos. SK* 28 *and SK* 27.

TODAY'S walk of $12\frac{1}{2}$ miles passes through interesting countryside coupled with extensive views. What more could a Peakland Wayer want? From Hathersage go past the post office to the minor road, turning left and walking along it for a short distance until you reach a small gate on your right. Pass through this and ascend the field to the graveyard of Hathersage church. Visit the church if you have not done so and leave it on your left, walking past the wall of the vicarage to the car park in front of the entrance. Here, on your right, you will see the stile and footpath sign. You walk a short distance straight ahead before descending to your left to cross a small stream and then bearing right across the field—you will see the stile in the top left corner. After this you keep close to the hedge on your left and follow a faint footpath to Cowclose Farm. Go through the gate before bearing right round the farm and later walking above the farm road to reach another stile to its right. Descend to the road before climbing this stile. At the "T"-junction turn left and after a short while turn right and ascend the path through Stanage Plantation to the top of Stanage Edge.

As you climbed the road you will have noticed the impressive looking building on your left, North Lees Hall. This is a small Elizabethan tower house built by the Eyre family; a date on the plasterwork inside the hall is 1594. The estate is now owned by the Peak Park Planning Board. Once on the top of Stanage Edge don't walk too far, but find a comfy stone with a good view and sit down and laze in the sun while you ponder on the geology of the Peak District. Having now seen the three major types of scenery of the Peak District—the limestone dales, the gritstone moorlands and the gritstone edges—let us look at their geology a little.

The Peak District is principally made up of two types of rock, gritstone and limestone, both of which belong to the Carboniferous System. The central region of the Peak is limestone country and is bisected by many limestone dales, such as Chee and Deep dale through which you have already walked. The rock's strata is saucer shaped and for this reason the limestone area is often referred to as the Derbyshire Dome. Flanking the limestone on three sides—the west, north and east—are the gritstone rocks. You were in gritstone country at Longnor and again on Mam Tor and Kinder, and the third side you are sitting on—the gritstone edges.

The limestones are the oldest exposed rocks in the area and were formed about 280 million years ago. The rock, which is on average 1,700 feet thick (except at Topley Pike where it is about 2,500 feet thick), was once the sea bed and is made up of sea creatures and shells. This is the reason why you find many fossils in the rock. Since it is soluble in water, the weathering agents have carved the limestone into the beautiful shapes we see today. The rock is also rich in minerals and in some places is 98% calcium carbonate. This accounts for the extensive quarrying you have passed on the Way.

The gritstone, which is known as the Millstone Grit series, is a direct opposite to limestone. Instead of being soft and easily weathered, gritstone is hard, coarse and impervious to water. Likewise it is a useful rock and is used as a building material. Until late last century, gritstone was used extensively for making millstones to grind corn. All the way along these edges which you will traverse today are numerous places where this rock was hewn into grind stones.

Stanage Edge, along with all the other edges, are popular rock climbing grounds and are the birthplace of British rock climbing that we know today. Renowned figures such as Joe Brown and Don Whillans learnt their craft here, raising the standard of climbing so as to equal and better the continentals. In 1956 the climbing guide to the edge detailed just over 200 climbs; ten years later a new guide was produced detailing some 450 routes. As you walk along you will be able to observe these human spiders as they climb the vertical and overhanging rock faces.

Walk along the edge all the way to Cowper Stone. On your left can be seen odd clumps of cotton grass—years ago the white fluffy heads were picked and used to fill mattresses and cushions and to make lamp wicks. Close to the path you will see the small yellow flower, tormentil, which you may have observed on each stage of the Way. The time to walk along the edges is in late August and early September when the surrounding moorlands are a blaze of purple from both ling and bell heather. It is a sight to gladden the heart of any traveller.

From the triangulation pillar, 1,500 ft., near the Cowper Stone, continue along the path and head down to the road near Burbage Brook and the entrance to the Burbage Valley. Of the many places seen on the Way, few will match this for quiet beauty. Flanked on either side with gritstone outcrops, a brook meanders down the valley which is carpeted with bracken and heather. On reaching the road follow it over the brook before turning right to walk down the wide grass track along the entire length of the valley—about 1½ miles.

On your right in the early stages is Higger Tor, which has gritstone buttresses adorning its southern side. One of the furthest ones is particularly notable as it leans from its base by fifteen feet. The buttress stands 45 feet high, and running up the overhanging face is a rock climb known as the "Rasp" on account of its rough nature. The climb is one of the hardest on gritstone and has only had a small number of ascents. Further down on your right is another hill surrounded by buttresses but of a smaller elevation. This is Carl Wark, whose summit plateau was used as a fort during the Iron Age in about 450 B.C. All that can be seen today is a wall at the northern end and a few boulders placed around the perimeter.

Well over a mile down the valley on your left are several abandoned quarries where you will find many discarded millstones. These reminders of the thriving industry that existed here and on all the gritstone edges, are mainly rejects. The stone was either dug or quarried before being hand-hewn into circular shapes. The principal use of the stones was for grinding corn but they were also used for pulping wood and crushing lead ore. A common size was 7 feet in diameter and about 12 inches thick, with a central hole. In 1815 the cost, in Hathersage, for a pair of 5 feet diameter stones was 10 guineas. Once the stone had been shaped it was paired for transport with a wooden axle; these were rolled down the slope and often travelled to their destination in this form. On other occasions the stones were loaded onto wooden carts. Many were sent abroad and were taken to King's Lynn in Norfolk for loading onto ships. By 1862 roller mills were being used to grind corn and this sounded the death knell of the industry, for it rapidly declined over the next few years.

On reaching the main road, A625, go straight across and through the small gate. Follow the footpath beyond for a short distance before turning left along the path to the gate and road (A6011) opposite the entrance to Longshaw. Cross the road and walk along the drive towards Longshaw Lodge—opposite the park gatehouse is a stone guidepost. Criss-crossing the Longshaw estate were numerous bridle-paths and roads, many of which are now lost, but from the stone to the right of the Longshaw Pool it is possible to trace the line of an old road. The guidepost has on its sides "Sheffield Rode," "Tideswell Rode" and "Hope Rode"—notice the old way of spelling road.

A little further along the road you come to Longshaw Lodge. Just before you reach the building you have to turn right, as signposted, and walk along the footpath beneath the garden wall. Next you go through a metal gate, and then immediately afterwards a white wooden gate, and continue along the grass driveway. Longshaw estate was owned by the Duke of Rutland, whose Derbyshire home is the renowned Haddon Hall near Bakewell. He used Longshaw as his shooting lodge, for he owned 11,533 acres of the surrounding moors—the largest moorland estate in the Peak District. The earliest known reference to Longshaw is in 1722 but, as it is on the boundary of Derbyshire and Yorkshire, writers on either county omit any reference to the estate which makes research a frustrating task. Building of the shooting lodge began in 1830, and over the next fifty years various Dukes of Rutland extended and enlarged the building. Here the shooting parties met during the grouse season, and on average 3,000 brace of grouse were shot on the nearby moors.

In 1927 the 9th Duke of Rutland divided the whole estate into lots and auctioned it all. The estate surrounding the lodge, which you are now walking through, is 750 acres in extent and was purchased by public subscription. The money took four years to raise, but in 1931 the land was handed over to the National Trust debt free. The house was used as a Holiday Fellowship guest house until the 1960s when it was converted into private flats.

From the white gate you follow a grass driveway all the way through the estate to the B6054 road, just over a mile away. It is one of twenty miles of driveways that the sixth Duke of Rutland constructed in the 1860s. He was a very keen sportsman and, although wealthy, he remained a bachelor. As a result he is often referred to as the "Sporting Duke" or "Bachelor Duke." Walking through the estate is delightful—bracken covers the floor, trees of oak and fir are set in small areas and rhododendrons are prolific, especially to your right around the pool. In due course you walk through the Sheffield Plantation. Sites of Iron Age settlements have been found here, but the plantation takes its name from the Sheffield Planting Company which was formed in 1823. It planted oak, fir, and silver birch trees on this 100 acre site. The company had been in existence for just over thirty years when the fifth Duke of Rutland purchased it in 1855.

At the end of the driveway you reach the road, B6054. Turn right and walk down it for just over half a mile so that you can go along the gritstone edges of Froggatt, Curbar and Baslow. By sheer chance everything works out well, for just after reaching the road you pass the *Grouse Inn* on your right. You are now half way through this stage of the walk, so a quick pint will not go amiss.

Refreshed, re-invigorated and not too light headed, I hope, continue down the road from the inn. Just after the road curves right you will see on your left the wide track which you follow along the top of Froggatt Edge. Walking along this edge is particularly fine, with the really thick heather blanket on your left. Opposite you have extensive views—the radio mast on Sir William Hill stands out predominantly, the limestone buttressed gorge of Stoney Middleton comes into view and a little further on you have wide vistas over central Peakland. Froggatt Edge possesses many hard rock climbs, but Curbar Edge—with which it merges— is known as the "Cloggy of the Peak." The buttresses tower up to seventy feet and all the climbs are of the highest order.

Some three miles from the *Grouse Inn*, and by now fully sober again, you descend to the minor road to Curbar. Go straight across, ascend the ladder stile and follow the wide track across Baslow Edge. Soon you will pass a large gritstone boulder on your left known as the Eagle Stone. The name is derived from the god named Aigle who is reputed to have been able to move boulders no man could lift. Walk beside the stone and head for the cross of Wellington's Monument, erected in 1866 to record the Duke of Wellington's visit to the moor as guest of the Duke of Rutland. Just over a mile away on top of Birchen Edge is another monument, to Lord Nelson.

By far the most captivating view of the whole Way lies before you at Wellington's Monument. Straight in front is the graceful valley where nestles the "Palace of the Peak"—Chatsworth House. Sit down and look at the scene for nowhere matches the serene beauty of this park. The left of the valley is wooded, the golden building lies in the middle, the river Derwent weaves its way through the park and the right-hand side is scattered with clumps of trees.

From the Monument descend a short distance on the path towards Baslow before turning left and following another path which curves left and drops down to the road, A621, beneath Gardoms Edge. Cross the road and go along the path which ascends the fields, heading to the right-hand corner of this Edge. Just over the top you descend to the A619 road. As you do so on your left is Birchen Edge and in front is Moorside Farm, your camping ground for the night. At the road turn left, then left again to the farm. That ends the sixth stage and the end of the gritstone edge walking. Moorside is a good place to stop with Birchen Edge closeby for exploration and a pub at the end of the track. Tomorrow, your last day in the gritstone country, and the day after—Ashbourne. Don't give up now; you have seen and toiled over many an interesting feature, and you are three-quarters of the way round.

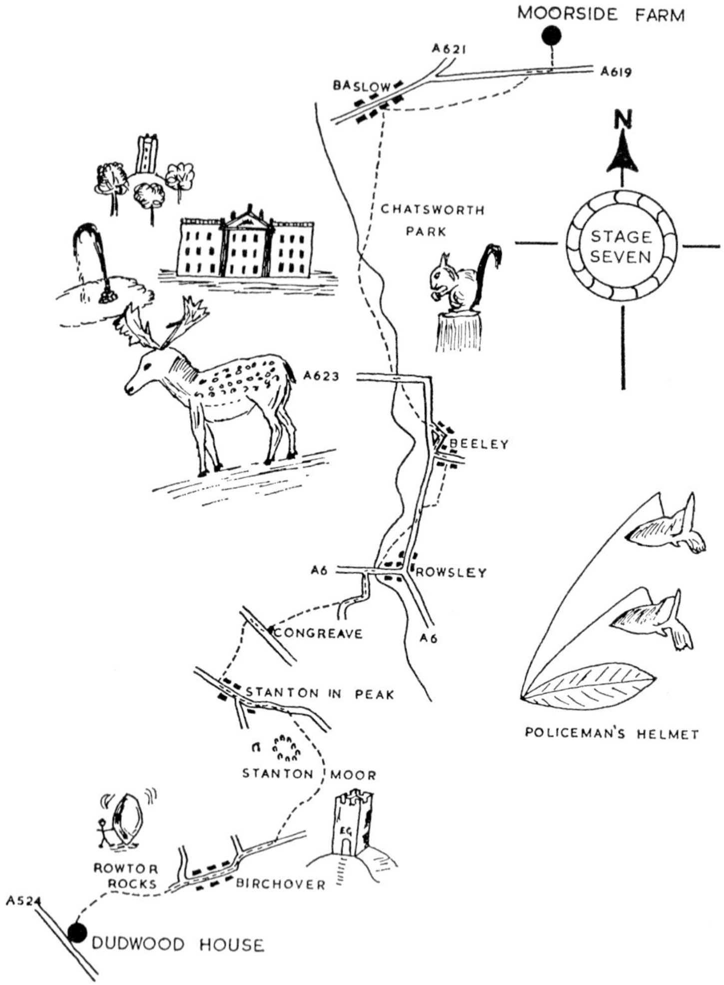

MOORSIDE FARM
A621
A619
BASLOW
STAGE
SEVEN
N
CHATSWORTH
PARK
A623
BEELEY
A6
ROWSLEY
CONGREAVE
A6
STANTON IN PEAK
POLICEMAN'S HELMET
STANTON MOOR
ROWTOR
ROCKS
BIRCHOVER
A524
DUDWOOD HOUSE

Stage Seven: Moorside Farm to Birchover

Route:-	*Moorside Farm — Baslow — Chatsworth Park — Beeley — Rowsley — Congreave — Stanton-in-Peak — Stanton Moor — Birchover*
Distance:-	11 miles
2½-inch O.S. maps:-	*Sheet Nos. SK27 and SK26.*

You are about to spend your last day in the gritstone country. Retrace your steps back down the farm track to the A619 road. Turn right and follow the road into Baslow, 1¼ miles away. Regrettably, there is no alternative to this short road walk at the time of writing. Leave the village by the track in front of the thatched cottage beside the stream, Bar Brook. Soon you come to a large metal kissing gate and once through this you enter the peaceful world of Chatsworth. First of all you walk through the trees where grey squirrels are often seen. Then you see the golden stone of the house in the nearby distance—it is a thrilling moment and the start of a three mile walk through enchanting scenery. If you want to give your feet a rest, walk barefoot through the park. The cool soil is invigorating.

The grass is a really lush green, the trees are artistically placed, the river swirls its way through, the house rests in the gentle curving valley and the absence of stone wall or fence gives the whole area a feeling of freedom. The house you see in front is in actual fact the second to be built on this site. Sir William Cavendish, the second husband of the redoubtable Bess of Hardwick, purchased this manor and a few others for £600 in 1549. Shortly afterwards Bess began building the first house which cost £80,000. Bess had a passion for building, her last work being the remarkable Elizabethan Hardwick Hall near Chesterfield. Her Chatsworth had just over a hundred years' life before being completely rebuilt in the style we see today over a period of the next 200 years. The only visible remnant of Bess's house is the shooting tower on your left, high on the valley side and surrounded by trees. From this four turreted building the ladies of the house watched the hunt or chase below.

The other original building is Queen Mary's Bower, which you pass on your left. Bess of Hardwick and her fourth husband, the Sixth Earl of Shrewsbury, were guardians of the unfortunate Mary, Queen of Scots, who on several occasions was "imprisoned" in Chatsworth House. The bower was surrounded by water and on top was a small garden where Queen Mary often spent her time during the day. If you ascend the thirty steps to the top you can see her coat of arms above the doorway. Just past the bower you reach the road, where you turn right and cross the three-arched bridge over the river Derwent. This was built in 1761 by James Paine. The corn mill and the houses of Chatsworth village were removed from here, so that the Duke of Devonshire had a clear uninterrupted view from the house. The mill was re-erected near Beeley and you will pass it in just over a mile.

While on the bridge it is worth admiring the house. Following his banishment from Parliament, the first Duke of Devonshire—as he became in 1694—spent the rest of his life rebuilding the house. Over the subsequent 200 years the other Dukes have carried on the work, culminating in the remarkable construction we see today. The Dukes are direct descendants of Bess of Hardwick and, while in some the passion for building lay dormant, others spent their entire life perfecting the house. On the far side of the bridge turn left and follow the path which later keeps close to the banks of the river Derwent. Often you will see the herd of fallow deer which roam in the park in this area. Further down you reach the ruined mill—the water channel can still be traced and the main wheel is still in situ. Carry straight ahead to the next bridge over the Derwent, likewise built by James Paine, and meet the main road through the park. Turn left and cross the bridge before turning right, as signposted, and following the path across the field to Beeley village on your left.

Cross the road and enter the village, passing on your left St. Anne's church, once a chapelry of Bakewell. The building dates back to the 12th century, but very little of the original remains because of extensive restoration work carried out in 1882. A glass case inside has the bassoon that was used to accompany the hymns before the organ was fitted. There are several memorials to the Saville family who purchased the manor at the end of the 16th century and lived in Beeley Hill Top house, half a mile north of the village. Just after the church turn right and walk past the houses to the *Devonshire Arms Hotel.* Many of the houses in Beeley were designed by Joseph Paxton, who was the gardener and friend of the sixth Duke of Devonshire. He was also responsible for houses in Edensor village, close to Chatsworth.

From the *Devonshire Arms*, turn left along the minor road towards Chesterfield. After about 200 yards turn right, as signposted, and follow the path across the fields. Stone stiles guide you until on reaching a wood after half a mile, you turn sharp right and descend through it to the A623. Here you are on the very edge of the Peak District National Park and you can see the park's mill-stone sign on your right. Turn left at the road, and just past a garage on your right you will see the footpath and sign—"Rowsley via Allotments." First you walk beside the river Derwent, then through the allotments and finally close to a small factory on your left before reaching the *Grouse and Claret Inn.* This stage of the Way is beginning to sound like a pub crawl—and there are more yet! As you walked over to here, you will have passed an abundance of purple pink flowers known as policemen's helmets, although correctly they are the Jumping Jack species of balsam. They grow along the bank sides and attain a height of six feet.

Just past the *Grouse and Claret*, you cross the bridge which, although widened twice, has five arches and dates from the 15th century. On the other side you come to the imposing *Peacock Inn* —yes, another! This was built in 1652 as a private residence for John Stevenson who was "man of affairs" to Grace, Lady Manners, the mother of the 8th Earl of Rutland. It was she who founded the Lady Manners School in Bakewell in 1636. Above the embattled porch is a stone peacock, which is part of the Manners coat of arms, and in the entrance hall is a very large china model of a peacock with long trailing feathers. Only five were ever made because of the extreme delicacy in manufacture; this one was removed from a sunken ship. When the other local inns—the *Nag's Head* and the *Red Lion*—closed down, the *Peacock* became the hotel in 1828.

While you are here it is worth walking up the road on the left of the *Peacock* to visit Rowsley church. Although it was built in 1855 it contains an impressive tomb to Catherine Manners, the wife of Lord John Manners. She died in 1859, aged 23, and later her husband became the 7th Duke of Rutland. Back at the *Peacock* again, cross the road and walk along School Lane. A quarter of a mile later, where the road begins to climb to Pilhough, turn right as signposted and ascend slightly to your left heading for Congreave. In the later stages you drop down through the right-hand corner of a wood before reaching the buildings. Here at the minor road turn right and descend for a quarter of a mile. On the level section of the road you will see the footpath sign, on your left, for Stanton-in-Peak. Turn left and climb through the fields—constantly in front of you is the spire of Stanton church.

You reach the village opposite the church. Although you probably won't see it, Stanton Hall was built by the Thornhill family in the 17th and 18th centuries. Over the door lintels of many of the village houses can be seen the carved initials, "W.T.", which stand for William Thornhill. The church, dedicated to Holy Trinity, was built as a private chapel for the Thornhills in 1837 and monuments to them can be seen inside. The predominant feature to see is the bronze Holy Water stoup, which was a gift from the Thornhills.

It is Venetian in style and, from the inscription on it, appears to have been cast by Antonio de Conti in 1596. Also to be seen is a barrel-organ, two small marble bas-reliefs and a tabernacle.

Continue up the road from the church through the village and keep straight ahead at the road junction. A quarter of a mile from here, at the end of the day's climbing, turn right as signposted and walk onto Stanton Moor. Shortly after gaining the moor the path divides. Take the right fork to visit the Nine Ladies stone circle, before retracing your steps to follow the left-hand path around the perimeter of the moor. The circle is 35 feet in diameter, has nine stones as its name implies and dates from the Bronze Age. Just beyond it is a wall surrounding a single stone, known as the King's Stone. It is believed that this was the male stone in the Bronze Age fertility worship. A more recent legend attributes these stones to a group of dancers and a fiddler who performed here on Sunday, causing an act of sacrilege. For punishment the dancers were turned to stone and likewise the solitary fiddler.

By walking round the left perimeter path on the moor you pass the Earl Grey tower, built by one of the Thornhills. Over the doorway can be seen a coronet and the inscription "Earl Grey, 1832," referring to the then Prime Minister and commemorating the first Reform of Parliament that year. From the tower you have an extensive panorama with Darley Dale in the bottom. Matlock is to your right with the stark brown walls of Riber Castle on the hill above the town, to your left is Chatsworth Park and in front are Holymoorside Moors. With such a view for company, walking along here is a pleasure. Rhododendron, heather and bracken cover the moor, which is at its best in August when the purple flowers are out and the bilberries ready for picking.

The moor also contains many burial mounds of the beaker people dating from about 1500 B.C. In each burial the person had a beaker placed beside him, and this possibly held alcohol to help him on his journey. Over seventy mounds have been located and many have been excavated. One notable burial contained a small urn, bronze dagger and flint scrapers, which can be seen in the Weston Park Museum in Sheffield. Continue round the moor's perimeter and, on reaching the road, turn right and descend into Birchover village. As you do so you pass the stone quarries on your right. The attractive light brown stone is very durable and is used for special buildings all over the country—the extensions to Sheffield Cathedral were made from it. If you pass the quarries during the week, you will more than likely see stone being cut with circular saws which are diamond-tipped.

Continue through the village until you reach the *Druid Inn*. Here you take the lane on its left-hand side, but before you do so it is worth visiting Rowter Rocks. The word Rowter is derived from "Roo", meaning to sway; there is a 50 ton boulder here which you can push with one hand and it will rock from side to side. The rocks contain passageways and seats, many of which were carved out by Thomas Eyre who lived below in Rowter Hall, now the vicarage. He made himself a study up here and did the carving for his friends to admire the view.

Descend the lane and pass on your left Birchover church, built by the same Thomas Eyre in 1700 as his private chapel. Beside the entranceway are fragments from the Norman church. Just inside the porch on the left wall is a plaque to Joan Waste who was burnt to death in the Windmill Pit in Derby in 1556. The pulpit was carved by the vicar, the Rev. C. W. Summerfield, in 1949. It took him two years, the base being from a tree trunk which grew in the vicarage garden.

Continue down the lane and, where this goes to the house on your left, follow a grass track. Keep straight ahead and contour round the hillside on the track. As you do so you will see the gritstone outcrops of Cratcliffe Tor on your right and Robin Hood's Stride on your left, both of which you pass tomorrow before entering the world of limestone. Part way round the hill the path descends to the road, but instead keep straight ahead and drop down to the farm which is your camp site for the night.

This is your last night on the Way—surely the joys and tribulations have been worth it. Just relax and if it is hot, similar to the weather I had on the inaugural walk, the cold water tap in the yard is too inviting. If you want a stroll after tea, a climb up to Robin Hood's Stride won't go amiss—it is an interesting place to explore at leisure. Tomorrow is your last day of the Way and the longest one!

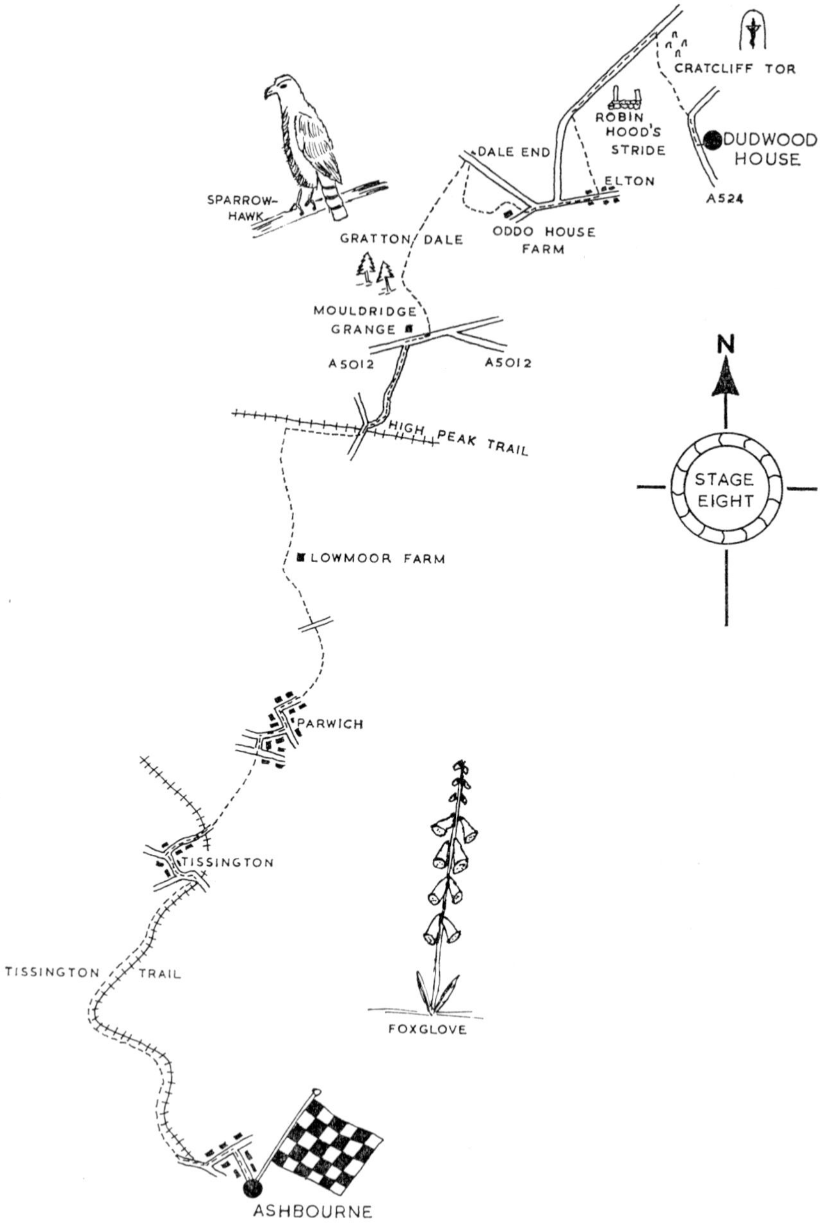
CRATCLIFF TOR
ROBIN HOOD'S STRIDE
DUDWOOD HOUSE
DALE END
ELTON
A524
SPARROW-HAWK
GRATTON DALE
ODDO HOUSE FARM
MOULDRIDGE GRANGE
A5012
A5012
N
HIGH PEAK TRAIL
STAGE EIGHT
LOWMOOR FARM
PARWICH
TISSINGTON
TISSINGTON TRAIL
FOXGLOVE
ASHBOURNE

Stage Eight: Birchover to Ashbourne

Route:-	*Birchover — Hermit's Cave — Elton — Oddo House Farm — Gratton Dale — Mouldridge Grange — High Peak Trail — Lowmoor Farm — Parwich — Tissington — Tissington Trail — Ashbourne.*
Distance:-	15 *miles*
$2\frac{1}{2}$*-inch O.S. maps:-*	*Sheet Nos. SK*26, *SK*25, *SK*15, *and SK*14.

THE final day dawns—the one you eagerly wanted at the beginning but now don't because you are enjoying things too much. The prize for making Ashbourne today is personal satisfaction, a steak well-done topped with succulent mushrooms, red wine, liquors, coffee, a cigar and . . . Oh, how the mind runs wild, but banish these thoughts for the moment and let us diminish the distance between here and Ashbourne.

From the camp site turn right down the road, and at the bottom turn left then right through the stile and ascend the grass track towards Robin Hood's Stride. This is a captivating slice of the Peak District and one that you never tire of seeing. Part way up the track turn right and walk past the cottage on your right before climbing to the base of Cratcliffe Tor. The reason for coming here is that on the left-hand side of the gritstone crag hidden behind a yew tree is a shallow cave. A wrought-iron fence guards the entrance and through the bars you can see a carved crucifix and rock niches. This was once a hermit's cave—the carvings are believed to have been done in the 14th century.

From the cave turn left and walk through the fir trees to Robin Hood's Stride. The uppermost part of this gritstone crag is adorned by two pinnacles, and the distance between them—22 yards—is supposed to be the same as the stride of Robin Hood. In the 18th century the group of rocks was often referred to as Mock Beggars Hall because of its shape and the way the pinnacles look like chimneys from afar. Just past the rocks the path bears right to the road opposite the entrance to Castle Ring Farm. As you walk along, over on your right is the Nine Stones Circle which dates from the Bronze Age. Only four stones comprise the ring but they are the tallest standing stones in Derbyshire. A fifth stone can also be seen and now serves as a gatepost. The area around these outcrops is ideally suited for stoats—often while walking here I have seen them running along the walls with their conspicuous black tails aiding identification.

On gaining the road turn left and follow it for approximately three-quarters of a mile. You pass a small quarry on your left, then the drive to Cliff Farm on your right and soon afterwards you reach the stile and footpath sign for the path to Elton village. You can see the gritstone stiles as you descend into a small hollow before climbing to the right-hand side of the church, built in 1812 after the original church steeple collapsed in 1805. The font is unusual as it has a stoup incorporated into the design. When the new church was built the old font was abandoned; later it was found in Youlgreave vicarage and placed in that church. It was then that the people of Elton realised their mistake, for the original font is unique. The Elton people were unable to get it back and so a replica, which you see today, was carved.

From the church, turn right and walk through the village heading towards Dale End Farm. Just on the outskirts you come to the driveway of Oddo House Farm on your left. Walk up here as signposted, "Footpath to Gratton Dale." After a few yards turn right, walk round the farm and guided by stiles descend into Gratton Dale close to Dale End Farm. In the bottom turn right to the farm and road, left at the road and left again almost immediately afterwards. Once clear of the farm's environment the walk down the dale is enchanting—you have now left the gritstone country for good and are back in the world of limestone. On my inaugural walk, as I passed the farm, I was mesmerised to see three young wrens sitting on the wall. Although I was only six feet away, they continued their wall hopping.

Further down the dale wood pigeons flutter and grunt in the trees, blackbirds and thrushes sing and fly from bush to bush and sparrow hawks criss-cross the valley in search of food. On the dale floor both red admiral and green-streaked white butterflies flit gracefully along from flower to flower. Gratton Dale may not have a river flowing through it, but it is very attractive and peaceful. Eventually you pass a small fir wood on your right, and just afterwards come to the end of the dale. Go through the gate and bear left around Mouldridge Grange, keeping close to a field wall and following it to the road (A5012) a quarter of a mile from the grange entrance. Turn right and walk along the road until opposite the drive to the grange where turn left and follow the minor road. After three-quarters of a mile this curves to the right beside the huge limestone embankment of the Cromford and High Peak Railway. A little further on, where the road crosses the course of the railway, you turn right.

This is the High Peak Trail and, like the Tissington Trail which you will encounter later in the day, is a disused railway line converted into a footpath. The Cromford and High Peak Railway linked two canals, the Cromford which was opened in 1792 and the Peak Forest opened eight years later. At first the plan was to have a canal joining the two but this never got off the ground. The railway was opened in 1830 at a cost of about £180,000 and the engineer of the line was Josiah Jessop. Because of the nature of the country, nine inclined planes were made on the line where stationary engines winched the trucks up. A passenger service was also provided but the railway was never a viable concern and ceased operating on 2nd October 1967. The line was opened as a public footpath in 1972.

Follow the trail for half a mile. First you walk through a wood and just afterwards you pass a small hollow on your left. On the right-hand side of this is a limestone stile in the wall. Here you turn left, cross the stile and walk through a field and then the arm of a wood before crossing another field to walk past the top right-hand corner of the same wood. Beyond this you reach a rough track—go straight across and continue over the fields to Lowmoor Farm. Many of the walls here have collapsed which means that the stiles are hard to locate, but as you near the farm they are made from wooden sleepers. On approaching the farm bear to the right round a small wood and pool before bearing left up the hillside where the stiles stand out prominently. Over the top you drop down to the minor road on the left of Hilltop Farm. This three mile section from the High Peak Trail to Parwich is one that is rarely trodden and, although you may not locate all the stiles, by keeping alert you should manage this section all right.

Cross the road—the stile is there—and begin to descend slowly and then abruptly as you bear right into Parwich. You should reach the village close to the hospital, although the path line does not exist. Walk through Parwich—one of the forgotten picturesque villages of the Peak District—and turn right to go past the church. This is comparatively modern, being built in 1873, but part of the original Norman building can be seen incorporated into the base of the tower. There is also a tympanum—one of the few examples in Derbyshire—and a Norman font. Just past the church keep straight ahead on the road, take the first road on your left and at the end of it, on your left, is the signpost and stile for the path to Tissington. Only about five miles to go now!

First you ascend the fields before dropping down and crossing Bletch Brook via a wooden footbridge. As you climb towards Tissington do turn round and admire the view back to Parwich. On your left and dominating the village is Parwich Hall, built in

1747 by Sir Richard Levinge. The manor was once owned by the Fitzherbert family who you will be hearing more about in Tissington. Next you ascend more fields; at the top is the Tissington Trail and the knowledge that all the climbing on the Peakland Way is completed. You cross the trail via the railway bridge. You can see the footpath below, but don't cheat—walk into Tissington village first and pick the trail up at the old station. You will soon see why, for Tissington with its hall, church and carefully planned village is a fitting sight for any traveller.

On arrival in Tissington turn left and walk through the village past the hall on your right and the church on your left. The manor of Tissington came into the Fitzherbert family at the beginning of the 17th century. Shortly afterwards Francis Fitzherbert commenced building the present hall in 1609, and the Fitzherbert family has lived here ever since. Opposite the hall gates is a well. There are five in Tissington, and the custom of well-dressing, dating back to 1350, commences here on Ascension Day each year. As a means of thanking the water-god, each well has a wooden frame erected over it. The frame supports clay boards and into this are pressed flower petals, bark, moss, corn and many other nature flowers to create a picture portraying a biblical scene or national feature. The art of well-dressing is unique to Derbyshire and is a very colourful display of an intricate custom of yesteryear.

A little further down the road you come to Tissington church—again a visit is a must. I know you are tired, but it would be a shame to miss this jewel of the Way. The church, dedicated to St. Mary, is of Norman origin, and the Norman font is particularly interesting with animals carved on its sides. There are many memorials to the Fitzherbert family, the most notable being to Francis Fitzherbert, the builder of the hall who died in 1619. His two wives are also included in the memorial as is his son who died in 1642. Opposite is a two decker pulpit which, following the last war, was converted to a single decker.

Follow the road round to your left from the church and walk past the pond on your right. Just after turn right and descend to Tissington station, car park for the Tissington Trail. Yes, my tired Peakland Wayer, the end is in sight. No more rooting for paths or looking at maps—just turn right and walk along the trail for a little over three miles to Ashbourne. Like the High Peak Trail, this is another disused railway which has been converted into a footpath. The line, which connected Ashbourne and Buxton, was made by Francis Stephenson for the London and North Western Railway Company and officially opened in 1899. It was closed to passenger traffic in 1954 and ten years later goods ceased to be carried, although part of the line remained operative until late 1967. The Peak Park Planning Board purchased the railway in 1968 and began the task of converting it into a grass track for walkers and pony trekkers.

The work completed, it was officially opened to the public on 5th June 1971.

As you walk along the trail you have a variety of flowers and birds to look at. Among the flowers you will see are red campion, dog rose, bindweed intertwining itself with other plants, common vetch, spotted orchid and rosebay willowherb. The trees are largely hawthorn, ash and sycamore, and fluttering around in them are numerous birds. These include magpie, mistle thrush, wren, chaffinch and yellowhammer and, near the village of Fenny Bentley on your left, I have seen both kestrel and grey heron.

Nearly there and nothing will stop you now! It can rain, it can thunder, it can even snow, but you will make Ashbourne. The tunnel is sighted ahead and the end of the trail—I can see a smile coming. At the end, turn right and then left and ascend the road. Oh, those corns: Turn left at the top along North Avenue, and then right down The Channel which you walked up a week ago when you set off. It's all downhill into the Market Place of Ashbourne. Just to prove you are fit, let's see you run. Pick your feet up, slow down for the road, then on to the cross. You've done it—my heartiest congratulations! Life goes on around you, but for you a glow of pleasure and satisfaction invades your body. You have just walked a hundred miles through an area of outstanding beauty and interest.

Knowing that it is all over, there are places to visit in Ashbourne such as the church and its monuments. But leave that for later. Find a cafe and let someone else do the cooking—you've earned a rest. If you return home tonight, have your sleeping bag beside the bed, for I know sleeping between sheets after what you have done is an experience. The bed's too soft, you feel cramped and have no sense of freedom. Well, Peaklander, I must leave you now. I am really glad you have made it and I am sure you will cherish the week's hardships for the rest of your life. Thanks for your company.

Part Two

Reference Section

Natural History on the Peakland Way

THE Peak District is rich in varied flora and fauna because of the area's geological make up. The following lists of both plant and animal life are from my own observations. I have not added any which I personally have not seen, believing in the maxim "it is better to talk about what you know". These lists barely do justice to the variety, and when you walk round the Way you will certainly see flowers and birds which are not included. Both flora and fauna vary with the month you are walking. During the year over 200 different species of birds are seen and the flowers are more numerous —one dale alone has over a hundred. Please observe the wild life but don't disturb it. Likewise, please don't pick the flowers—just admire them.

BIRDS

Moorland

Red Grouse
Meadow Pipit
Golden Plover
Dunlin
Skylark
Ring Ouzel
Wheatear
Curlew
Twite

Gritstone Country

Tree-creeper
Great Spotted Woodpecker
Whinchat
Common Sandpiper
Ring Ouzel
Wheatear
Meadow Pipit
Curlew
Grey Heron
Starling
Chaffinch
Bullfinch
Sparrow-hawk
Crow
Wren
Blue Tit
Great Tit
Robin

Long Tailed Tit
Greenfinch
Skylark
Coot
Rook
Pheasant
Wood Pigeon
Song Thrush
Magpie
Linnet
Moorhen
Blackbird
Cuckoo
Black Headed Gull
Mistle Thrush
House Sparrow

Limestone Country

Tree-creeper
Nuthatch
Wheatear
Curlew
Kingfisher
Dipper
Grey Wagtail
Mallard
Tufted Duck
Little Owl
Robin
Redstart
Sedge Warbler
Redpoll
Swallow
Pied Wagtail
Wren
Blue Tit
Great Tit
Moorhen
Coot
Blackbird
Raven
Lapwing
Fieldfare
Lesser Black Backed Gull
Marsh Tits
Bullfinch
Hawfinch
Wood Pidgeon
Whitethroat
Yellowhammer

FLOWERS

Moorland

Ling
Cowberry
Crowberry
Butterwort
Sphagnum Moss
Maidenhair Spleenwort Fern
Bilberry
Cranberry
Bog Asphodel
Round-leaved Sundew
Cotton Grass

Gritstone Country

Bilberry
Wood Sorrel
Bluebell
Hard Fern
Wavy Hair Grass
Ling
Eyebright
Devil's Bit Scabious
Sheep's Sorrel
Tormentil

Sheep's Fescue
Common Bent
Mat Grass
Purple Moor-Grass
Heath Bedstraw
Red Campion
Lesser Celandine
Poppy
Clover
Snowberry
Sneezewort
Marsh Thistle
Meadowsweet
Policemen's Helmet
Gorse
Periwinkle
Marsh Marigold
Foxglove
Honesty
Yellow Loosestrife

Limestone Country

Meadow Cranesbill
Dog's Mercury
Ramsons
Wood Anemone
Arum
Butterbur
Wood Sorrel
Herb Robert
Ground Ivy
Wood Forget-Me-Not
Crosswort
Lesser Meadow Rue
Bloody Cranesbill
Mossy Saxifrage
Sheep's Fescue
Slender Bedstraw
Devil's Bit Scabious
Milkwort
Carline Thistle
Cowslip
Early Purple Orchid
Jacob's Ladder
Mountain Pansies
Scurvygrass
Male Fern
Coltsfoot
Rosebay Willow-herb
Ragged Robin
Lady's Smock
Knapweed
Gorse
Blackthorn
Marsh Marigold
Ox-Eye Daisy
Bluebell
Primrose
Lilly of the Valley
Mountain Melick
Wood Sage
Greater Burnet Saxifrage
Globe Flower
Nettle-leaved Bell Flower
Musk Thistle
Marjoram
Thyme
Harebell
Rough Hawkbit
Small Scabious
Kidney Vetch
Rock Rose
Eyebright
Clustered Bell Flower
Hawkweed Oxtongue
Grass of Parnassus
Birdsfoot Trefoil
Germander Speedwell
Monkey Flower
Hart's Tongue Fern
Twayblade
White Dead Nettle
Yellow Archangel
Meadow Buttercup
Great Hairy Willow-herb
Watercress
Red Campion
Lesser Celandine
Foxglove
Clover

Yellow Stonecrop
Goatsbeard
Rattle
Limestone Fern
Stitchwort
Bugle
Dog Rose
Tufted Vetch

TREES

Turkey Oak
Holm Oak
Sessile Oak
Hawthorn
Yew
English Elm
Wild Privet
Holly
Beech
Scots Pine
European Larch
Silver Birch
Rowan
Hazel
Ash
Sycamore
Lime
Elder
Sweet Chestnut

FUNGI

Fly Agaric
Honey Fungus
Ink Cap
Dryad's Saddles
St. George's Mushroom
Fairy Ring Champignon

BUTTERFLIES

Gritstone Country

Meadow Brown
Wall Brown
Green-streaked White
Small Tortoiseshell

Limestone Country

Common Blue
Painted Lady
Brown Argus
Red Admiral

MAMMALS

Mountain Hare
Hedgehog
Mole
Common Shrew
Water Shrew
Bat
Grey Squirrel
Bank Vole
Water Vole
Weasel
Stoat
Red Fox
Badger
Fallow Deer
Rabbit
Red Squirrel
Field Vole
Brown Rat

Places of Interest on the Peakland Way

The following notes are a brief summary of the principal historical places you pass on the Way.

CHURCHES

Ashbourne—Dedicated to St. Oswald. The spire, 212 feet high, is said to be "the finest single spire in England". North transept has tombs to the Cokayne and Boothby families. Penelope Boothby tomb of particular note.

Mapleton—18th century aisle-less church, with pillared porch and lantern topped dome.

Ilam—Built in 1611. Several Saxon crosses in graveyard. Inside is St. Bertram's tomb, two funeral garlands and Chantry's statuary to David Pike Watts, a former owner of Ilam Hall.

Longnor—Classical style with a false ceiling. Graveyard contains grave to William Billinge who died aged 112.

Earl Sterndale—Built in 1828 and has interesting stained glass windows.

Wormhill—Tower a copy of the Saxon tower at Sompting in Sussex. William Bagshaw, the "Apostle of the Peak", preached his first sermon here in the 17th century.

Peak Forest—Built in 1880 replacing chapel which was built in 1657. Font shaft can be seen in graveyard. The Reading Room adjacent is built from the chapel's stone. The place where runaway marriages were solemnised between the years 1728 and 1754.

Hathersage—Graveyard has tomb to Little John. Inside are many brasses to the Eyre family, once principal landowners in the Hope Valley.

Baslow—Spire has two clocks, one with Roman numerals and the other saying "Victoria 1897". Inside are colourful stained glass windows, a pitch pipe for tuning the organ and a dog whip.

Beeley—Largely rebuilt in 1884, but contains a Norman doorway and 14th century tower. Inside are memorials to the Cavendish family.

Stanton-in-Peak—Formerly a private chapel for the Thornhills of Stanton Hall. Inside is a 16th century Holy Water stoup and Florentine Quatrocentro tabernacle.

Birchover—Small chapel built in the early 18th century. Inside doorway on left a plaque to Joan Waste, burnt to death in Derby in 1556. Pulpit carved by the vicar in 1947.

Elton—Built in 1812 following the collapse of the earlier church's steeple. The font, which includes a Holy Water stoup, is a replica of the original now in Youlgreave church.

Parwich—Present church dates from 1873 replacing Norman one, of which a few remains are incorporated into today's building.

Tissington—Norman doorway, tympanum and font. Beautiful stained glass windows and tombs to the Fitzherbert family, the owners of the hall and village.

HALLS

Ilam—Built about 1842 in Victorian Gothic Revival style by Jesse Watts Russell. Given to the National Trust and now serves as a Youth Hostel

Throwley—Forlorn ruins dating back to 1603, in front of present hall.

Wormhill—Elizabethan and owned by the Bagshawe family who have been associated with this area for centuries.

Wheston—Now a farmhouse. Parts of it date from the 17th and 18th centuries.

North Lees—One of the seven halls of the Hope Valley. Built by the Eyre family probably in 1594—a date found on the plaster-work.

Longshaw Lodge—Former Dukes of Rutland shooting lodge. Building started in 1830 and added to over the years. Now converted into private flats.

Chatsworth House—"The Palace of the Peak". Home of the Dukes of Devonshire. Present building was created between the years 1700 to 1850.

Parwich—Red brick hall built in 1747 by Sir Richard Levinge.

Tissington—Begun in 1609 by Francis Fitzherbert. Extensively enlarged and altered in the late 19th century.

INDUSTRIAL ARCHAEOLOGY

Mapleton Mill—Watermill with the water wheel in the centre.

Coldwall Bridge—Formerly part of a coaching road and dating from 1726. A milestone on it records "Cheadle 11 miles".

Manifold Valley—Footpath follows line of the Leek and Manifold Light Railway. Work began in 1902 and line officially opened on June 27th, 1904. Financially a disaster; was closed in 1934 and converted to a footpath.

Wettonmill—A corn mill which ceased operating in the late 19th century.

Ecton Hill—The copper mines here were very active in the 18th and 19th centuries. In 1760 the annual profit was in excess of £10,000. Mining ceased in late 19th century.

Brund Mill—A corn mill in 1760 and later used for cotton spinning. During the second world war it was used for grinding corn. The water wheel is in the centre of the building.

Hathersage—In the 18th and 19th centuries a principal place for the manufacture of needles. Several won silver medals at the Paris Exhibition. Industry ceased late last century and many buildings still remain.

Gritstone edges—Once the scene for a prolific industry in millstones. Many imperfect stones still remain scattered along the edges.

High Peak Trail—Part of the Cromford and High Peak Line. Built by Josiah Jessop and opened in 1830. Last section closed in 1967. Converted into a footpath and opened to the public in 1972.

Tissington Trail—Part of the Ashbourne to Buxton Line. Designed by Francis Stephenson for the London and North Western Railway Company and opened in August 1899. Passenger services ceased in November 1954. Converted into a footpath and opened in June 1971.

ANCIENT MONUMENTS

Ilam—Saxon cross shafts in churchyard and on Paradise Walk.

Beeston Tor—St. Betram's cave where fifty Saxon coins were found in 1924. Lynx and Lower Lynx Caves where bones from pole-cat, reindeer and lynx have been found.

Thor's Cave—Occupied in the early centuries A.D. Arrow heads, bone combs, iron adzes, spindle wheels and bronze armillae have been found. This area of the Manifold Valley has numerous archaeologically interesting caves, namely Wetton Mill Minor Rock Shelter, Mill Pot, Darfur Ridge Cave, Ossom's Cave, Old Hannah's Cave, Thor's Fissure Cave, Seven Ways Cave and Elder Bush Cave.

Thirst House Cave in Deep Dale—Excavated last century. Finds included Roman remains and pieces of early pottery.

Wheston—15th century cross, twelve feet high. The finest cross in Derbyshire.

Windy Knoll Cave, near Mam Tor—Excavated last century; yielded 6,800 bones and 500 teeth.

Mam Tor—Iron Age Fort. Hut foundations found in 1965 date from 1,180 B.C., the late Bronze Age.

Edale Cross—Wayside preaching cross on highest point of track between Hayfield and Edale.

Doctor's Gate—Roman road built about 78 A.D. linking the Roman fort of "Melandra" at Glossop and "Navio" at Brough in the Hope Valley.

Carl Wark—Iron Age fort with defence wall along its western approaches.

Froggatt Edge—Bronze Age stone circle.

Stanton Moor—Nine Ladies, Bronze Age stone circle. Numerous burial mounds of the beaker folk, all over the moor's top.

Cratcliffe Tor—Hermit's cave, occupied in the 14th century, has a crucifix carved on the back wall. Behind the Tor is Nine Stones circle, of which only four stones remain in situ.